DATE DUE		
JAN 2 9 '72	JUN 1 1 1976	
FEB 2 0 '72	JUL. 2 1976	
MAR 10 '72	JUL 23 1976	
JUN 13 '72		
JUN 27 '72	DEC. 1 1 1976	
	JUL. 1 1 1977	
APR 6 '73/	OCT. 1 1977	
DEC 17 '73		

*How to Invest
in Beautiful Things
Without Being a Millionaire*

How to Invest
in Beautiful Things
Without Being a Millionaire

How the Clever Consumer
Can Outthink the Tastemakers

by

Elaine Cannel

DAVID McKAY COMPANY, INC.
New York

HOW TO INVEST IN BEAUTIFUL THINGS
WITHOUT BEING A MILLIONAIRE

COPYRIGHT © 1971 BY
Elaine Cannel

Design by C. R. Bloodgood

LIBRARY OF CONGRESS CATALOG CARD NUMBER: 75-157938

MANUFACTURED IN THE UNITED STATES OF AMERICA

Acknowledgments

A book of this kind, reporting as it does on the good taste marketplace, is not a simple matter of news coverage. Many people in the course of many years have contributed to the information contained herein. It is impossible to acknowledge the help of all of them by name, so only a partial list of acknowledgments follows: Marshall Arko; Rita Battistini; Robert Brennan; Julia Child; Donald Claflin; Stirling Callisen; Ralph Chait; John Daley; Bernard Dannenberg; Barbara Donovan; Bruce Dorfman; Abe Feder; Sidney Feltman; Lawrence Fleischman; Maurice Freeman; Bess Myerson; Chaim Gross; Judith Gura; Charles Hicks; Elinor Hillyer; John M. Hogan; Diana Jacobs; Judith Jones; Carl Joseph; Carol Klein; Eleanor Kluger; Jack Konner; Rae Sprigle Kurland; Kenneth J. Lane, Edward Munvis; Elizabeth Meehan; Jacques Mourlot; Barbara Pallenberg; Kay Pinney; Francis X. Pollock; Michael Ponce de Leon; Sarah C. Rabinowitz; Ernest Reuter; Alexander Schaffer; Martin Stansfield; Otto Spiekermann; John Thomas; Gilbert Thurston; David Webb; Hans Weinberg; Arnold A. Wolf; Joan Zimet.

E. C.

Contents

Chapter III

FURNITURE   37

Do Decorators Help? . . . What You Should
Know About Prices . . . Plastic Furniture
(Polystyrene, ABS, Polyester, Acrylic, Poly-
propylene, Polyurethane) . . . Solid Wood
. . . Veneer . . . Inlay . . . Carving . . .
Finishes . . . Fittings . . . Legs . . . Drawers
. . . Upholstery . . . Reproductions . . .
Upkeep and Refinishing . . . Outdoor Furni-
ture (Rattan, Wicker, Wrought Iron, Alumi-
num . . . Redwood) . . . Strapping and Lacing

Chapter IV

PAINTINGS, PRINTS AND SCULPTURES   61

The Nonsense of the Art Market . . .The Art-
By-The-Yard Business and How To Detect It
. . . How To Spot Facsimiles . . . How To Buy
a Painter—Not a Painting . . . All About
Prints . . . Woodcuts . . . Engravings . . .
Mezzotints . . . Etchings . . . Lithographs . . .
Silk Screens . . . Sculpture—Marble, Bronze,
Stone, Reproductions

Chapter V

CHINAGLASS   88

How To Play the China and Glass Market
Wisely . . . All About Pottery—Ceramic,
Earthenware, Ironstone, Stoneware, Faience,
Majolica . . . Crystal—Cut, Lead, Colored . . .
Glass—Handblown, Pressed . . . Mirrors—
Antique, Venetian, Chock, Plate, Mercury,
Frames . . . Collecting Glass

Chapter VI

Chapter VII

Chapter VIII

Chapter IX

---▸◂{ Contents }▸◂---

*How to Invest
in Beautiful Things
Without Being a Millionaire*

I

Investing As It Relates
to Beautiful Things

*I*T was a typical suburban commuter's house, looking just about the way it did ten years ago when the last owner bought it: three bedrooms, two baths, a garage, and a Yorkshire terrier barking in the quarter-acre yard.

In short, it was an average $24,000 house as these houses go. And as these houses go, it went for $56,000 last month. And as for the Yorkshire terrier, she cost $125 ten years ago. But her great-grandchildren and their puppies sell for upward of $300 each.

I mention these transactions because this is a book about investing, although not in real estate or livestock. It is a book about investing in beautiful things. So it is quite important at the outset to define that word "investment," a word that involves so many other words, such as "market," "manipulation," "money," "madness," etc.

Investment usually implies buying and selling for profit. And anybody surveying the market these days, from houses and dogs to paintings and sterling silver, would have to conclude that that definition still holds true. Since 1960, the sales price of the good life is up from 30 to 120 percent. At least that is how it looks generally speaking.

But except for real estate and pedigreed dogs, there is an enormous difference between the selling price and the re-selling price.

For example, a 3-carat diamond ring that sold for $2,900 ten years ago sells today for about $3,700. But if it's your ten-year-old ring, you probably can't resell it for much more than $1,500 in the jewelry market. A service for twelve of sterling silver flatware that sold for $475 when it was new in 1960 sells for about $600 today. But if you are selling it, don't expect a dealer to offer much more than $250. The Oriental rug business is booming in new, used, and antique models. A new Sarouk that sold ten years ago for $1,000 sells today for $1,600—unless it's yours. If you are reselling it, the transaction probably won't bring you more than $375.

There are, of course, very good reasons for this difference between the sale and the resale price. For one thing there is the whole matter of style and the way it changes year by year. Ten years ago pear-shaped and emerald-cut diamonds were in fashion. Today it is the marquise that leads the demand. In addition, the settings for gems have changed. The chances are that in a decade yours has gone out of fashion. Sterling silver, on the other hand, has not changed much in style. But then, neither has the rate of production. Your secondhand set may be in excellent condition. But it is still secondhand in a market brimming with new. Furthermore, the market is made up of various sales prices that depend only on who is doing the selling. There is the manufacturer's sales price to the wholesaler, the wholesaler's sales price to the retailer, and his price to you. Everybody has to get his share, or there would be no production and very little distribution. The retail price of a rug is roughly twice the whole-

sale price. And the resale price by the owner is roughly half
of the wholesale price—a very uncomplicated formula, and a
great time-saver for all the people in the professional market.

In addition to the machinery of style, fashion, and
production-distribution, there is also the mechanism of merchandising that helps keep the resale price down. Let's face
it: your dining room table simply doesn't look as good in
your home as it does in the window of an austere and elegant
showroom. Moreover, when it comes to wooing a buyer—or
even finding one—you can't begin to compete with an established dealer. His know-how, location, and daily traffic are
worth money.

It is also necessary to mention the touchy subject of
quality in explaining the difference between selling price
and reselling price. Quality is a very curious matter. It frequently means little in the sales price, but shows up like a
neon sign when it comes to a resale. Take that $2,900 3-carat
diamond ring of ten years ago, which sells for $3,700 today
but resells for only $1,500.

"It's only an average diamond," one of the leading gem
merchants told me. "And average diamonds seldom appreciate in value because there are so many of them. Only the
really fine stones can be resold at a profit by their owners. A
really fine 3-carat ring would have sold for about $12,000 in
1960. You could resell it to me today for around $15,000."

Well, how does all of this affect a working definition of
investment in beautiful things? There are several obvious
answers to the question.

First, there is a difference between investing for profit
primarily, and investing in something to live with, enjoy,
and grace your existence with. Investing primarily for resale
and profit is the calling of the professional.

But second, there is no reason why your purchase price

should go down the drain, or be amortized away through use. An Oriental rug if it is fine quality is not to be compared with fine granulated sugar. That means the best investment is usually the best quality, the admission that you are paying the top price, and the knowledge that it will probably command the top resale price if you decide to part with it.

In that regard, when it comes time to resell, don't be in a hurry. Shop the market and find out what the going selling prices are, and—if you can afford the time and energy—try to make a private sale. If the matter is more urgent and you sell to a dealer, get several estimates, in several cities, if possible. And if you can bear to wait, try to get a dealer to take your items on consignment. In that way he will take either a percentage of the price, or any amount he can get over the price you want. But recognize that he must make a commission for his service, overhead, and clientele developed in years of doing business.

There's another generally used meaning of investment that requires some translation for use in the market of beautiful things. In common parlance, investment frequently implies a supply-and-demand mechanism, a sort of seesaw balanced between what's available and what people need or want. The more scarce such an item, the higher its price.

Now that kind of working definition certainly applies to much of the market in beautiful things. Rembrandt painted only so many pictures, and he's not going to paint any more. So his masterpieces bring millions of dollars to investors. This same kind of investment in collectors' items can be applied to the porcelain market, too. For example, for a month or so last year a showcase in a large New York antique store displayed a bone china seal about a half-inch high, made in England in 1770 and marked at $450; a finely made Meissen statue of Venus, about 1880, selling for $25,000; and a pair of Italian figures that appeared to have been made by an apprentice porcelain worker on his first day on the job. But, being the only Capo-di-Monte pieces of their kind on record, they were marked $29,000. So scarcity and demand make up the investment market in porcelains, too. And being highly breakable, the supply gets scarcer with time, while the demand grows ever greater. There is no love like the love of a porcelain collector for his specialty.

Well, it may not be possible to get any new production out of Rembrandt. But it isn't terribly difficult to make a rare piece of porcelain. All you need is a sculptor to make the molds, the kaolin-and-petuntse mixture to pour into them, the kiln to fire the finished pieces, and a sledgehammer to break up the machinery when the run is finished. This process is known as the limited edition. It usually means 500 pieces at the very most before the molds are destroyed, insuring that no other pieces of that run can be made again.

And so, to meet the demand with a profitable short supply, the porcelain industry has created something new under the investment sun—the Instant Antique or the Immediate Collector's Item. "It is a very attractive item no matter how you look at it," says a spokesman for one of the largest and best-known china companies in the world. "With a limited edition, the pieces are immediately rare so a store can almost guarantee that a purchase will be 2 or 3 percent more valuable as soon as the buyer takes it home.

"Moreover, there is no risk about the authenticity of the piece. Even the most untrained eye can see what it is. And, of course, with instant antiques the price is within everybody's range."

A few manufacturers don't like the idea—but only because of practical considerations. Says an executive with one of the oldest English china companies: "We are getting a line of limited editions ready, of course. It's the new prestige line and we have no choice but to go ahead with it.

"But I don't mind telling you that we'd rather not. It's terribly expensive and time-consuming. Not only the actual designing and production, but also all the nonsense about a big ceremony afterward when you break up the molds."

On the investment side of the market, this instant antique was greeted with approval. One collector, who specializes in old Meissen and Sevres, told me that "this sort of thing is pretty much an American invention. Europeans would be aghast at the idea of an immediate collector's item. But I buy these new pieces occasionally. Some of them are quite good." And, added another investor in the porcelain market, "At their best, these new pieces are as good quality as most of the finest porcelain ever made. And as long as they are original pieces making a statement about today and not trying to masquerade as antiques, I think it's all right."

Under the circumstances, it is not surprising that a number of other manufacturers have joined the instant antique market. As a look at the advertisements, especially around Christmas, will tell you, there are now immediate collectors' items available in items ranging from whiskey bottles and cosmetics jars (filled with the product, naturally) to machine-made reproductions of great paintings and statues. And they all fill the requirements of a working definition of investment in the market. They are rare and scarce in supply. And there is a demand, at least for things on which they are patterned. As to the quality of these instant antiques, there is no doubt that they are technologically perfect.

But how do they really fare on the market?

In some cases, such as whiskey bottles and facsimilies of

paintings, it's still too early to tell. In some cases, quite well.
A pair of porcelain quail made by American sculptor Doro-
thy Doughty cost $275 when new in 1940 and were sold last
year for $36,000. And in some cases, not so well as the instant-
makers had told their prospective customers. A pair of 1935
Doughty birds that went at auction last year for $3,800
brought only $1,700 at a similar auction this year. But in any
case, it's a hothouse market and it depends on a good deal of
outside pruning and mulching to keep it in full flower. So,
for the buyer who sees it as a way not only to art and decoration but also to growth and profit, there are a few words of
caution:

This is a professional's market, reserved for the dealers,
collectors, and other investors who understand the machinery at work. If you buy an instant antique, buy what you
like—most especially if it contains whiskey or face cream.
Look for craftsmanship, detail, artistry; but don't start
counting any porcelain chickens.

While the Iron Curtain remains closed, beware of recent pieces marked "Meissen" or "Dresden." We don't trade
with that part of the world, and the chances are not great
that the pieces are actually made there. If, however, those
labels were applied only as a bit of added glamor under a
glaze applied in Newark, New Jersey, forget the whole thing
as an investment. Even if the market in immediate collectors'
items goes up, it's quite likely that these won't be among the
rising throng.

The Immediate Collector's Item is only one new way
that supply has been increased to meet demand in the market of beautiful things. There are two additional inventions
that have been brought out recently to serve the same pur-

pose, and these indicate still another change in the definition of investment. To wit:

Airport Primitive

A look at much of the art and object-of-art market today reveals the remarkable fact that if a thing is made of clay, wood, glass, or canvas, then it must be art. And if it's art, then there must be a buyer. Almost to a man, the art, antique, and secondhand merchandise dealers report that this market is enormous. Or it would be if there were anything left to sell. But in the first-rate painting division there isn't much around. At least not at a reasonable price in the galleries. The well-known painters and schools of painting bring millions of dollars. And then, they're only to be had at auctions. So if a gallery gets a Renoir, for example, it's frequently either a third-rate example of his work or else it's a scrap from his studio. But even that commands top prices.

"As a result," says a leading art dealer, "everything is in today. Anything goes—because there's nothing much to sell."

Under the circumstances, the market fills and empties with everything else. It's not put in those terms, of course. To hear many vendors and wholesalers talk, you'd think it was simply the latest development in the evolution of civilized man. For example, one dealer said solemnly: "We are having a long overdue revival of nationalistic art: the French, the English, the American, the German schools are finally being recognized for the truly beautiful works they produced. Nobody is buying Impressionists anymore." And from another dealer: "We are no longer emotionally antagonistic to rural life. We have come to recognize the farm and pastoral values for what they are in true perspective. In addition, we are terribly upset by problems of urban life, like overcrowding . . ."

Translation: There aren't any Impressionist paintings to buy. And so all of those old barnyard scenes, apple-and-pear still lifes, and scenes of peasant maidens dancing about the Maypole that haven't been seen outside of the junk shops for 50 years or more are available at reasonable prices.

Or at least they have been. For some time now they have been in short supply, too. The invention of such styles as Pop and Camp, added to a growing popular demand for original painting, have helped to empty the market of even barnyard scenes. And so, as art—like nature—abhors a vacuum, the galleries are stocking primitives.

Strictly speaking, primitive art is not art at all. In its native habitat it is a very useful article like an arrow or a shield or an idol to pray to for rain and a mask to wear while doing so. Just what it says to a modern, urban American is quite hard to figure out. But whatever it is, an authentic rain god goes for about $100 today. A pregnant stork made of straw and used in fertility rites is a bit more—$1,200.

Art like that being invested in, it is not surprising to find primitives manufactured in places like the Congo, Haiti, and Tahiti expressly for the American market. And at rather reasonable prices, too. At the present writing the market in airport primitives is doing quite well.

Attic Recent

At every lecture on antiques there is always a group of questioners wanting to know what their antiques are worth—an old silver thimble, an old tortoiseshell shoehorn, an old pressed glass bowl that grandma got for her soap coupons. It used to be easy to parry this sort of question without using the word "antique," simply by asking in return, "Do you really want to sell your heirlooms?"

But that is no answer in today's market, where the word

"antique" covers everything from a Paul Revere piece of silver (if you can find one) to a 1939 box of Gold Dust Cleanser (at $6 as of last Friday). These days it is sentiment that brings the prices once reserved for antiquity. And it's not hard to see why. The prices of traditional antiques have been skyrocketing in the past fifteen years. A sterling silver bread tray that sold for $35 when it was new in 1880 and for $95 in 1950 now sells for $350. A cut crystal decanter in the same period has gone from $25 to $175. A set of English flatware made in 1860 sold for $1,800 five years ago and is up to about $4,000 today. There are hardly any complete sets of old china to be had at any price. Nor any sterling silver coffee service trays. Nor old candlesticks, unless you're willing to buy them in sets of four.

But there seems to be something about the civilized human that cannot live without antiques or heirlooms somewhere in his setting. Even the Romans collected Greek antiques, and the Greeks collected Etruscan antiques. And today, with this century's antique depositories either emptied or out of reach, the vacuum has become filled with what can best be called "Attic Recent." But even that Attic Recent is growing thin.

Within the past decade the market has seen the return of the colored glass lamp shade popularized by the Tiffany Studios around the turn of the century. This sort of shade couldn't be given away 25 years ago. But today a Tiffany-style model is up to $300, and the real one can go for as high as $3,500 or more. Golden oak furniture, new at the turn of the century, has returned, too—with much more pomp and circumstance than it ever knew in its original setting in the farmhouse kitchen and sitting room. A kitchen table that might have brought as much as $5 in 1950 is up to about $200 now. An old kitchen chair has jumped in the same period from $1 to $50. A four-drawer kitchen cabinet has gone from $15 to $150 in these two decades.

And now, with Attic Recent being bought up, and old Helmar cigarette boxes going for $4, and new Tiffany-style lamp shades in production again, it's difficult to say what an old thimble or shoehorn or soap-coupon pressed glass bowl will bring. And as for the working definition of the word "investment," it may well have to include such items as last year's used Christmas cards and this year's calendars (with or without illustrations).

The word "investment as it is generally used also implies a value that can be ascertained by a consultation with the market. A share of stock, for example, or a used car has a worth that can be appraised in this way at a moment's notice. But in the world of beautiful things, this definition requires a bit of adjustment, as the following real-life illustration will show.

The scene was a jewelry shop. And after inspecting the small sapphire pin, the jeweler said, "I can give you $300 for it."

"That's absurd," the woman snapped. "This pin has been appraised at $2,200. I have the appraiser's letter right here."

"In that case," the jeweler said with a sweet smile, "I'll give you $310."

Examples of pedestrians who fall into the appraisal machine fill the notebooks of any reporter who regularly covers this market in beautiful things. There is, for another, the case of the TV executive in a fury over an heirloom teapot. He had sold it for its appraised value of $500, only to discover that it had been resold for $850. There is the instance of a woman who had lost her diamond wedding band after 30 years of marriage (and 30 years of paying insurance premiums). But because she couldn't prove what the ring had cost originally, the insurance company appraised the loss at half of the insured value.

It's not supposed to work that way, of course. In theory, you go to an expert in rings, pins, or teapots. And for a fee, he tells you what yours is worth. But in real life it doesn't work out that way. Appraisal of value is much more like an open manhole into which you throw your cherished possessions, and hope they are still there when you want to recover them. The problem in having an object appraised boils down, finally, to the simple question of "What is it worth to *whom?*" To apply that question means considering "to whom" before getting an object appraised. For example:

What is it worth to an *owner?* Less if he has to sell it. More if he wants to replace it. Less if he has to pay tax on it. More if he wants to donate it for a tax deduction.

What is it worth to an *appraiser?* His fee depends on the value of the object. So he makes more money on a sapphire pin worth $2,200, and less on one worth $300.

What is it worth to a *merchant?* Less when he buys it. More when he resells it. In any case, it's worth what the market will bear.

What is it worth to the *market?* More if it's in short supply. Less if it's out of style. A newly discovered vein of amethyst in South America a few years ago has changed subsequent appraisals of that gem. And if it is in a setting that has gone out of style, the old appraisal is probably even less valid.

What is it worth to an *insurance company?* More if the policy covers an object appraised high. Frequently less if the company has to pay on a loss, and you have only the appraisal and not the original bill of sale to prove the object's worth.

Under the circumstances, it's often hard to ascertain true market value in the world of appraisal. And in addition, there is also the constant jeopardy of outright fraud. It is not unknown in the district attorney's office for a retail store to be in collusion with an appraiser. "You're getting a real bargain," an unscrupulous merchant will say. "But don't take my word for it. Have it appraised . . ." And with that, he will suggest an appraiser or two. Beware of such suggestions.

Finding an appraiser on your own can be a problem, too. Experts are not born, they are made—and sometimes out of nothing more than a business card and a letterhead. But even training and experience are not necessarily a guarantee. The Gemological Institute, for example, teaches its students how to grade diamonds. But a spokesman concedes that the Institute has no control over its graduates after they go out on their own. On the other hand, the Appraisers Association of America chooses its members on the basis of their ethics and personal dealings. But this organization has only 600 members.

What can you do to protect yourself and your investment when it comes to getting an appraisal? Only a few things. But they're better than nothing.

Beware of offers of free appraisals. Beware of stores that recommend appraisers. Save your sales slips—all of them. And in cases of very expensive objects, have a photo taken of each. When it comes to picking an appraiser, an executive at Cartier puts it this way: "You go about it the same way you'd go about picking a doctor."

The matter of insured value has difficulties all its own. Once upon a time—and not so long ago, either—people were frequently heard to say, "Oh, well, it's insured . . ." But not anymore. These days the problem with insurance frequently comes to not whether you can collect for some part of your loss, but whether you can get insurance compensation or even any coverage at all. Just how bad this situation is cannot be reported accurately because no insurance company queried on the subject would answer any questions or even discuss the general picture. But a continuing random sample of insurance brokers and premium payers sheds quite a lot of light on the problem.

The wife of an auto company executive says: "I haven't worn my jewelry in years. It's simply too much trouble to go down to the bank and take it out, give my insurance agent the required advance notice that I'm going to do so, and get it back to the bank vault within the required time period. I wear costume jewelry most of the time. It's a lot easier all around."

An insurance broker who supports two homes, two boats, and two families on his commissions says: "For heaven's sake, don't quote me by name. But the fact is, the insurance companies are impossible to do business with when it comes to collecting on a loss. Most of them are very busy trying to raise their premium rates, without dipping into the profits they make on their investments to help keep those rates down. If you have a theft or loss, you may either have to go to court to collect, or else you may find yourself submitting overblown, dishonest estimates of your loss in order to collect a portion of what they're really supposed to be."

Depending on the law of the state, an insurance company can cancel its coverage following a loss or when the policy comes up for renewal. And if you reinsure with another company, they may demand that you take out a $1,000-deductible policy. For most people, that's like paying a full premium for half coverage. So, when it comes to investment, the definition needs some reworking. No matter what its appraised or insured value, if it's too hard to enjoy it and still stay within the terms of the policy, what is it really worth?

That's not an insoluble problem. Far from it. But it does require some fortitude to overcome it.

First, you have to bow to the fact that every man is a corporate entity these days. As in the case of appraisal, you absolutely must save all of your bills for everything and, if you can stomach it, a notation of every expenditure you make. If you have articles you value, including costume jewelry, get yourself a small safe or sturdy steel cabinet with a good lock. It may not keep a persistent burglar out, but it will show evidence that he forced his way in. In addition, keep an inventory of all of your valuables, preferably in a safety deposit box or bank vault (the cost of them being tax deductible).

But just as important, if you don't like the treatment you're getting from your insurance company, complain to your state agency that regulates this industry. And complain immediately and repeatedly.

It should go without saying that your insurance company is just that—yours. But sometimes they forget that. A man who lost a suit of clothes in a fire, and then spent months in correspondence and conversation with his insurance company in an effort to collect, reports the following dialog with an executive of the firm:

"I'm sure you can understand our delay," the insurance company man said. "We've got to be careful of how we disburse our money."

"It's not your money," the premium payer said. "It's my money. I've been paying it to your agent for 25 years."

"Yes. Well," the executive said after a pause, "will you settle for 50 percent of the cost of the suit?"

This word "investment" also implies a marketplace where things change hands for a price. And that definition holds firm and true in the world of beautiful things.

There are three places where these transactions usually take place. And a few words are required to explain them.

First there is the shop, store, gallery, or studio run by a

dealer. If you're investing via this marketplace, don't try to look like a know-it-all, even if you know more than the dealer. If you've got the facts on your side, let him do the talking and asking, and then counter with your heavy guns and make him the offer you want. It's surprising how often this kind of tactic wins reductions in asking price. If, on the other hand, you don't have the knowledge, the dealer will find it out as soon as you start talking. The disadvantage is on your side then, and you have become fair game. But in either case, you cannot begrudge his commission or profit. There is a cost in doing business, especially high in this kind of retail business where there's no telling how long you have to wait to match an item with a buyer's needs.

The second marketplace where beautiful things change hands for a price is the auction. Of all the national sports, nothing comes close to the auction. It is dramatic. It is a fight to the finish. And any number can play. In the past five years the number of auctions in the United States—from gallery to barn—have quadrupled, which is more than you can say for the number of ball parks, stadiums, theaters, and TV stations.

But it is not the simple sport it appears to be. For one thing, there is no guarantee that the prize on the block is what is seems to be. Many a sow's ear has gone for silk purse prices, because auction houses are not required to take responsibility for what they sell, not even the houses with the best reputations. Moreover, there is no way to tell whether the bidding is really competitive. A spirited bidder may actually be working for the auctioneer. He in turn may be announcing bids higher than those he really hears. Or the owner of the item on the block may call it back rather than let it go for what the bidding has offered. For all that, however, it's still possible to get a good buy at an auction if you will just keep in mind the name of the game and what the score is.

1. If it's a perfect day for an auction, stay home. The best weather for an auction is a record snowstorm or intolerable heat and humidity. This usually means the house is small and the bidding low. A rainy day, on the other hand, frequently draws a big crowd.

2. If it's a single owner's collection for sale, stay home. For some reason, the possessions of one owner usually bring more money than an auction of items from many sources. The theory seems to be that if one person collected this assortment, he must have known what he was doing. Don't bet on it. But don't bid on it, either, if you're looking for a bargain.

3. If it's an auction at a private residence, stay home. First, because it falls under the single-owner difficulties. And second, because it often doesn't. The estate on the block may really be what the owner left. But the chances are that it will have been supplemented for the occasion by items the auction house has supplied.

4. If you've "just got to have" a certain item, stay home. Or else walk out when it comes up, and leave instructions with your spouse or a friend on how high to take the bidding. Otherwise, it's odds-on that you'll get carried away and beyond when the bidding starts, especially if the piece is expensive.

5. When the bidding starts, don't look up. If you want to play the auction game successfully, you'll keep your eyes on your catalog, your notebook, or your fingernails. It's the only insurance you've got against being overwhelmed by the prize and the other players. After all, an auction house is designed to overwhelm you or disarm you. Auctioneering is showmanship, plain and simple. And it's quite easy to follow the lead of dealers or other bidders who appear to be experts.

But just what they know, and just why they're buying, isn't usually self-evident. And those pieces on the block, even if you've seen them at the exhibition before the action begins, will never look so good as they do under the hammer.

The third marketplace for beautiful things is the show or fair. These have the advantage of gathering many dealers and their wares in one location, a great saving of time and energy. But frequently a sizable addition to price.

For one thing, it costs dealers quite a bit of money to come to shows and fairs: travel, moving, insurance, etc., as well as room and board during the stay. These costs may be added onto the price tag. But there are several other reasons why prices at shows appear to be rising. In their own words, here are the remarks of several dealers at a big show in western Pennsylvania recently:

An Ohio dealer: "Most of my business is with other dealers at these shows. We end up buying and selling to each other and driving the prices crazy."

A Philadelphia dealer: "A lot of the trouble is you reporters. You go around these shows and write down the prices of everything you see. Then people see what you've said, and come out here to sell us their things at retail prices. If we need stock, we have to buy. But we have to add in our profit, so the price goes up higher—and then you come around and report it. You're informing people right out of the market."

A porcelain purveyor from Massachusetts: "All sorts of people come to these shows, and a lot of them go home figuring that they've just seen a good way to make a living. Suddenly shows are twice the size they were last year or the year before. With more dealers in the business you'd think the prices would come down because of the competition. But it works just the other way. A hardware salesman becomes an antiques dealer, buys a Faberge clock from me for $2,500 and then puts it on sale at a show for $12,500. It's absolute madness."

And from a New York dealer: "I only play the largest shows these days, and then only as a sort of institutional advertising campaign for our store. I come in with a handful of very rare and expensive items and sit with them and read or chat with passers-by. I don't expect to sell anything because most shows today are either flea markets with broken glass, telephone insulators, and 1945 gin bottles for sale, or else they're public exhibitions where people come to look, ooh and aah, but not to buy."

In this swirl of prices and dealers and merchandised nostalgia or snobbery, it is still possible to find a bargain. But there are a few things to keep in mind in the show circuit. First, don't insist that an object be signed by the maker. Signatures cost plenty, and sometimes they're not real. Second, watch the crowds and see whether they're buying or looking. If they're not buying, make the dealer an offer of real, modern American currency. He may be in dire need of a sale—any sale—to bolster his morale. And third, get the dealer's name and the address of his shop. It's often easier to talk turkey when you get him away from the show where he won't be feeling so awful about having wasted his time and money to set up a booth.

Now, about that most common of all implications in investment—that value rises inevitably as time passes. That is just as true for beautiful things as it is for common stocks.

In December of 1967 a sterling silver coffeepot made in England during the reign of George II sold for $1,500. A pair of candlesticks of the same material, origin, and age went for the same price. By 1970 that coffeepot was on sale for $1,000, and the candlesticks for $1,200.

In 1967 an eighteenth-century English sofa table sold for $1,650. In three years the price was down to $1,000—or less if you wanted to take the time to bargain with the dealer. And so on and on.

But there are three footnotes to that market report for investors in beautiful things.

➤First, the market in top-quality objects has not fallen a bit. On the contrary, a pair of English commodes of the George I reign sold recently for $37,000, which is $4,000 over their price in 1969. This rising trend can also be seen in sales of medieval tapestries and masterpiece paintings.

➤Second, there is no real, reasonable way to compare the market price of a fine Oriental rug, say, with the price of a share of stock. In the words of one rug dealer: "It's silly to try. I put my money in rugs because I have to have merchandise to sell. But if I were a customer, a rug is the last thing I'd think of as an investment, even if I knew I could sell it for a profit. I can see buying a rug as a way to add warmth and elegance to my house. I can see it as a thing of beauty. I might even see it as a work of art. But you've got to be a little nuts to see it as something to produce income for your old age."

➤Fad objects and those touted by many financial writers as "a good hedge against inflation" haven't done well, particularly in the antiques department. One of the best-known investment columnists in the papers devoted quite a bit of space a couple of years ago to the portfolio advantages for the "careful buyer . . . in Empire furniture or old flags with historical significance . . ."

Between the time that column was written and today, most Empire furniture hasn't moved up one dollar in value.

And regarding the investment in old flags with historical significance, one specialist in that market recalled the column and its consequences with a broad grin, saying: "We had quite a run on old flags for a while. But actually we didn't sell many after we explained to everybody that 'historical significance' means unquestionable proof that the pennant under consideration had been carried by Custer into battle, or had flown from a mast on Old Ironsides."

For the kind of investor in beautiful things who takes this as bad news about the state of the market, there is a ray of hope. As of this writing, a spot check of dealers indicates that a boom may be building in old carved-wood duck decoys —$25 four years ago, $100 to $125 now. If the trend continues, to coin a phrase, it ought to be in the financial news pages by next month at the very latest.

II

Silver

THE elegantly dressed woman in the elegant store was looking for a gift—"Something in silver. A platter, I think."

"Certainly," the salesman said. "Plate or sterling?"

"Oh, plate would be fine," the woman replied. "Just as long as it's very heavy. This is an important gift."

Well, there is very little you can do for people like that. She does not really know the difference between sterling silver and silver plate. And she will not ask. No matter how much money her ignorance wastes, she simply will not ask. The whole subject of quality and taste completely overawes her. She is easy pickings for the interior decorator and self-assured salesman. And quite needlessly.

There is no reason why the eighth-grade class in home economics should not be taught the different meanings of such words as sterling, plate, coin, Sheffield—along with such words as baste, hem, and sift. It's time that America got over its self-consciousness and fear in the presence of the good life. Besides, knowing the terms used in silver is simply a matter of self-protection. Most of them define the amount of the pure precious metal that by Federal law must be used in the manufacturing process; so learning the language is a big step toward getting your money's worth.

Solid silver. A metal precious to art, craft, and industry, and consequently in shorter and shorter supply these days. Depending on the minerals market, an ounce of solid or pure silver can cost from $1.29 to $1.89. But solid silver is too soft to be used in tableware without the addition of other, harder metals.

Sterling silver. In the United States and England this term means that the item has been made of 925 parts of solid silver per 1,000. The remaining 75 parts may be tin, copper, nickel, etc. In France the highest grade of silver contains 950 parts of the pure metal per 1,000. In either case, the heavier the object, the more value it has for its precious metal content.

Coin silver. As the name implies, a standard used in minting money. In American colonial days, that meant about 900 parts of pure silver. Coins being about the only source of silver for colonial smiths, much early American work was done in this metal. When the great U.S. silver mines were discovered in the West a century ago, the age of using coin silver came to an end.

German, European, Continental silver. These terms almost always mean that the object contains less than the 925 parts of pure silver per 1,000 that is required of sterling in the United States. German silver can contain as little as 800 parts, and is sometimes called "eight hundred silver" in the market. What Continental silver pieces lack in the precious metal, however, they often make up in brilliant craftsmanship. But because of the lower silver content, they generally command lower prices than coin, sterling, or French highest quality.

Sheffield. This was the first successful plating process. It put objects made of some silver, at least, into homes of average families who could not afford the price of sterling. Basically, Sheffield is a sandwish made by rolling a sheet of copper between two sheets of silver. It was made only from about 1750 to 1850, and Sheffield design and craftsmanship are among the finest silver work in the world. The old, real Sheffield is a collector's item today—even if it has worn thin and the copper shows through in places. In fact, an aged and worn piece of original Sheffield loses a great deal of its value on the market if it is resilvered.

New Sheffield. A plated silver made since 1850, which does not command the respect or price of the old. The glamour of the name "Sheffield" can confuse the unsuspecting investor. Unlike old Sheffield, which was made by a rolling process, new Sheffield is electroplated.

Electroplate. Or, in modern times, silver plate. Electroplate was the successor to Sheffield, the silver being put on the base metal by an electric and chemical process. In plate, the thickness of the silver is measured in molecules. So, the heavier the piece, the more base metal has been used—not silver. Unlike Sheffield, electroplate that has worn thin and black can be replated with no loss in the resale value of the piece.

Vermeil. Sterling silver with a coating of gold. The process used mercury as an agent to bond the two precious metals, and is no longer legal because of its lethal hazard to workmen.

Gilded silver. Also generally sterling silver with a coating of gold. This process uses copper as the bonding agent and is still in operation. In vermeil, the mercury no longer remained once the coating was finished. In gilded silver, the copper stays sandwiched between the silver and its gold outer coat.

Looked at in black and white, there is nothing magical or mysterious about those terms. And the same is true about the hallmarks used on silver. But as any antique dealer or writer on the subject can testify, hardly a day goes by without a query or two from people who—well, here is a typical letter from a family in Pennsylvania:

"We have an old tray that has been in the family for a long time. There are hallmarks on the back of the tray. Can you let us know how valuable it is?"

It is not always a tray, of course. Sometimes it is an old spoon or fork, a teapot, a locket. In one instance it was a piece of broken Wedgwood cup. But in every instance there are hallmarks. And to judge by these queries, the general theory seems to be that hallmarks are some sort of magic marking that give great worth to an ordinary object—or even a broken piece of it. How this mystique came about is impossible to say. But it is part and parcel of the same costly awe that surrounds most matters of art and taste, especially when antiquity and handwork are attached to the object. In the cold light of day, however, making a mystique of hallmarks is about the same as looking for mystery and magic in a label that reads: "Made in U.S.A. Patent Pending. Guaranteed Waterproof."

The hallmark actually began in England some 600 years ago as the official stamp placed on gold and silver articles at Goldsmiths' Hall. The stamp usually gave the following information:

(1) That the metal had been tested for purity and did in truth contain 925 parts of pure silver in 1,000 parts of the finished product. (2) That the test had been made at this or that particular Goldsmiths' Hall, in (3) this particular year. (4) And that the tax, if any, had been paid by (5) the maker. Naturally that is a lot of information to put on a sterling silver spoon handle, for example. So hallmarking

used an agreed-upon set of symbols for each item—stamps of animals, letters of the alphabet, flowers, castles, crowns, and the like. In time, this system was adapted by other countries, which naturally set up their own standard symbols. To take one hallmark—the symbol for sterling: the British have used the stamp showing a lion since the thirteenth century; the Americans have used the stamped word, "Sterling," since 1861; and the French highest grade of silver, which contains 950 parts of pure metal per 1,000, is hallmarked with the head of the goddess Minerva.

Just where the magic in this stamping lies is questionable. But there is certainly a persistent mystique about it. And as you might expect, unscrupulous manufacturers have capitalized on the matter through the years.

Porcelain and pottery were never required by any law to be tested for purity. And neither were old English silver plate or Wedgwood. But many makers of those objects began to employ hallmarking for both identification and status value. And eventually much of their work was copied by imitators and counterfeiters who merely forged the "hallmarks" as part of the day's work. As a result, the marks on old porcelain frequently are a jumble of meaningless marks which require an expert to decipher. Old Sheffield may or may not have hallmarks, depending on how the manufacturer felt about having them at the moment. On old electroplated silver, the marks have a way of looking remarkably like those on sterling.

On the other hand, real hallmarks don't guarantee great value, either.

For one thing, in times of great affluence it has not been unknown for some silversmiths to cut old hallmarks from small objects—card trays or lockets—and put them on new, large expensive serving platters or tea trays. But even if the marks haven't been altered, they can't make a poor piece of craftsmanship better. Nor can they fight the fashion that makes a big part of the market. A teapot made by Hester Bateman in 1792 is worth about $1,000 today. The same kind of teapot made by her sister Ann, working at the next bench at the same time, is worth only about $350.

And just to make the picture complete, some of the most valuable articles have no hallmarks at all. Colonial American regulations did not call for a maker's identification, a purity test, or a Goldsmiths' Hallmark at all. And so a fellow like Paul Revere, who had quite a few irons in the fire besides his silver smelter, signed his work only when he had the time.

There are two cautions here for the wise investor in silver. First, if you're in the market for the old and antique—whether it's sterling or not—acquaint yourself with the dictionary of hallmarks. There are several good ones in the bookstores. Learn how to use the book, and take it with you when you shop. And second, whether you're buying old, new, plate, or any other kind of silver, make sure you get a signed statement from the dealer, spelling out exactly what you've brought from him, what it is, when it was made, and by whom. Even if it's for silver plate, it's a nice piece of paper to have if and when you decide to cash in on your investment.

Now, that is not to say that dealers are out to misrepresent or bilk. It takes only a few defrauded customers to ruin a shopkeeper's reputation in this market, and he knows it. Unlike the grocer, who bears no responsibility for selling foods made with additives, or a car dealer whose wares are unsafe at any speed, the vendors of beautiful things are staking their personal integrity and expertise on each sale. A gravy boat, if it is sold as old, real Sheffield and turns out to be ordinary electroplated silver, cannot be sent back to the factory and replaced under the terms of the warranty. If the dealer has said it was Sheffield—and said so in writing—the problem is his to solve. It is his name that is on the line, not Sheffield's. And it is the buyer's responsibility to keep it there. Expecting it to work any other way is like—well, here is a perfect example out of real life:

A recent advertisement in the newspaper read, "We Buy Old Sterling Silver." And the market being what it is, the store was packed with people who had come to sell. But for quite a few, it didn't work out that way.

One woman, who had brought her ensemble of silver tray with three matching crystal and silver whiskey bottles, was going home with them again. And very angry about it, too.

"I bought this set in 1929 for $200," she told me. "You'd think they would be worth three times that now, if not more, with the price of silver what it is today. But these cheapskates offered me only $200 . . ."

A man who was leaving the store with his silver tea set unsold stopped to growl an answer to my question:

"I think this operation is a real fraud. Here's a magnificent Victorian silver set. These people admit that it's magnificent. But they won't offer me a penny for it. What's going on here anyway?"

What was going on there was not the procession of misrepresentation these people thought it was. Rather, it was an example of what happens to buyers who have not fulfilled their responsibilities in the market.

That woman's set of crystal and silver whiskey bottles on the tray, for example, was plainly stamped "EPNS"—initials that stand for electroplated nickel silver. So it wasn't sterling at all, and it isn't worth a penny more today than it was when it was new 40 years ago. And as for that magnificent Victorian sterling tea set, it is sterling without a doubt. The hallmark of the lion attests to that. But the hallmark next to it says that it was made for the coronation of Queen Elizabeth II, a half-century after Queen Victoria's time. Why the owners of these articles didn't know that is simply because they didn't ask. And it never occurred to them to find out the meaning of the stamps and hallmarks on the pieces, or to get their pedigrees in writing at the time of the purchase.

To expect that the dealer buying old silver will tell them is plain foolishness. In the first place, as any old horse trader knows, it's the seller's responsibility to know what his merchandise is worth, and the buyer's to get his money's worth. But there's more to it than that in the workings of the market where a shopkeeper's reputation is at stake with each sale. The man who had advertised to buy old sterling puts it very neatly:

"Everybody in this business is everbody else's competitor. But we have to stick together for protection. If you tell a customer that what he bought last year as Victorian sterling is really Queen Elizabeth II, you're actually accusing the dealer who sold it originally of being unscrupulous. And you don't do that because first of all it may not be true, and second because you don't want him to do that to you."

In addition, says another dealer in silver who specializes in old rather than antique items, "People don't necessarily want to know the reality of the situation. Many of them would much rather be sold romance—and boy! they're sold just that. A regular customer of mine came in with a purchase she made in Europe: a sixteenth-century Wedgwood plaque. Now, it's not really my business to point out to her that Wedgwood didn't exist until the eighteenth century. And besides, what good would that information do her? She didn't buy that plaque to resell it. She bought it to hang on her wall.

"And anyway, if I told her the truth, I would have embarrassed her by pointing out her ignorance and her irresponsibility. And that's a sure way to lose friends and antagonize customers."

But knowing the difference between sterling and coin, and between buying and selling, are only part of knowing how to invest in silver. It is equally vital to understand how the market in this area of beauty works. Of all the transactions in the taste exchange, silver has a particular attribute to reckon with. After all, even the sleekest car is traded in after a few years. The loveliest dress can be out of fashion in a matter of months. Crystal crashes and china chips. But—alas—sterling silver is forever.

At least that's how a number of silver companies see it. And after years of watching how styling, fragility, and planned obsolescence work their magic for the rest of the good taste industry, the sterling silver people in some firms have been looking for a route to the paradise of turnover. If one of these plans being tried out works, it will be a triumph of Yankee Ingenuity over both good sense and good taste.

According to this plan, you bring in your old sterling flatware to the store, and the store replaces it piece for piece with new flatware in the pattern of your choice—at half price. Eventually your old silver finds its way back to the factory, where it is melted down and the metal is used again to make new flatware.

Looked at in this way, it seems a reasonable enough market operation—certainly a fairer deal for the customer than the clothing market gives him. Nobody has ever expected Coco Chanel to offer a trade-in on last year's suit. But viewed more closely, the trade-in plan in silver tells the investor some interesting—and profitable—things about the market. To begin with, there are the silver pieces that have been brought in for trading. Only the factory sponsoring the plan knows the whole picture, and they are reluctant to talk about it. But a buyer at one store participating in the trade-in reports:

"We see some pretty remarkable stuff come in. A complete set of old Gorham Chantilly pattern, for example. It must be at least 60 years old."

His counterpart at another participating silver department says: "We're getting commemorative and souvenir spoons on trade-ins, as well as real old heirloom pieces. These things would probably bring a good price in the secondhand and antique market."

Pressed on that matter, the company sponsoring the trade-in plan agrees that some of the pieces brought in have considerable value in resale. "But," says a company spokesman, "it would simply not be fair to the customer to make any use of these traded-in pieces other than to melt them down."

One of the nation's largest dealers in old and antique silver laughed heartily when that remark was repeated to him. "Of course they're melting the stuff down," he said. "The whole idea is to turn owners into consumers. And you can't do that by letting their trade-ins recirculate in the secondhand market. The whole problem is that sales of old silver are cutting into the sales of the new. If you want an active market, you've got to take the old out of circulation permanently."

Now, there are a number of advantages for the wise investor in this trade-in plan, especially if it becomes an industry-wide program. For one thing, it is a great escape hatch for today's bride who is urged at every turn to furnish her home completely before she knows what she likes. As one bridal consultant puts it, "It is very comforting to a newly-wed to know that she will not have to live forever among her mistakes." And for matrons whose taste has changed over the years, or who have become more affluent, the chance to trade in old silver patterns is a good opportunity to clean out the attic without taking a total loss on the enterprise. For both bride and matron, the risk of trading in something very valuable is not terribly likely. Since 1942, most sterling made in the United States has been of one weight—and not particularly heavy, either. So the intrinsic value of the silver metal is not likely to be awfully high.

Before 1942 most companies turned out sterling silver in several weights for each pattern. The chances are that this older silver may be heavier than the new, and so worth more, ounce for ounce of pure silver. And as the old and secondhand silver market is cleaned out, it may be advantageous to sell rather than trade in for new. It is also important to remember that the price of all silver, old and new, has been climbing steadily during the past fifteen years. In 1952, for example, a five-piece dinner setting of Chantilly cost less than $30. Today, that same setting newly made costs well above $70. So the careful investor has to do a little remembering or research to find out what the trade-in is actually costing. An outright sale on the secondhand market may be more profitable. And under the circumstances, a buyer looking for a set of flatware ought to investigate the secondhand market, too. Increased activity there is luring all sorts of things out of mothballs at prices that have to compete with the new, as well as with the antique.

That is very hard advice to follow, I know. For some reason, the idea of new or antique is very acceptable, whereas the mention of secondhand floats on the distinct odor of disreputability. Why that is so is almost impossible to explain, when a fork made during the reign of King George I is in no better condition or operation or purity of metal than a similar tool made during the reign of George V. But the fact is that it does work that way, and so do the new, secondhand, old, and antique silver markets. Between those two forks lies a gap of 200 years and, in the proper setting, $75. But it's not necessary to look back that far to see the mystique of antiquity.

Late Victorian home decoration—the kind of thing so

authentic that eminent Victorians wouldn't have had them in their homes—are now bringing record prices simply because there isn't much else to buy in the antique market these days. For example, an 1890 secretary that sold for $35 in 1954 is now bringing about $1,500. A turn-of-the-century bridge lamp that gives just enough light for a one-club bid wouldn't have brought a nickel on the market 25 years ago when it was only old. Today it is an antique and goes for $700. But nowhere has the spell of antiquity been more magical than on the pitted patina of Victorian silver plate— which is really electroplate, not even Sheffield. Scarcity and ridiculously high prices in antique sterling and old Sheffield have managed to make plated lead and tin into what ought to be called "instant heirlooms."

Ten years ago, when there was still plenty of old and antique sterling around, Victorian plate was kept in out-of-the-way showcases for customers who didn't know any better or didn't care. Ten years ago a Victorian sterling coffee service sold for about $700, and its counterpart in plate for about $300.

That has changed in this past decade. By last year the showcase had been moved to the front of the store, where a Victorian plate coffee service sold for about $900 (and its counterpart in sterling was up to about $2,300 if you could have found one to buy). A Victorian plate stuffing spoon was up to $35 (while the sterling variety was up to $80). And so on. But no increase of price can change the fact that it is electroplated, and that the veneer of pure silver is less than paper thin. Nor does this kind of booming market cover up the poor workmanship of much of the plate produced during the Victorian era when the process was in its experimental stage and base metals, such as lead, were frequently too heavy and awkward to be beautifully wrought, or, like Brittania metal, too soft to take intricate designing.

Investing in silver because it is antique only is a hazard-

ous route. If it is truly an investment and not just a speculation, you have to have a well-developed eye for excellent
workmanship as well as the expertise to be able to know that
the base metal is either copper, which can hold good design,
or nickel, which is intrinsically more valuable than the other
base metals usually used in Victorian plate. Sooner or later
the market always shakes itself out, and the good investment
usually proves to be the most beautifully made piece of the
most precious metal.

But even when there is no question about the intrinsic
value of the metal, antiquity is still not enough to insure a
good investment.

True enough, the 1960s saw the overall price of antique
sterling climb tenfold. Between 1964 and 1968 the prices
leaped 300 percent. But suddenly in the summer of 1969
antique sterling silver on the London market dropped 40
percent, followed by a decline in auction prices in the
United States.

Now, that does not mean that *all* antique silver fell in
price. Only the run-of-the-mill and second-rate old pieces lost
value in the market. In cold cash, that meant that an English
George II coffeepot which went for $3,700 the winter before,
to break an auction record, brought $1,600 six months later.
And an American sterling bread tray of the Grover Cleveland era fell from $375 to $185 during the same period. And
for run-of-the-mill investors in silver, it came as a great surprise to find out that the designations of "antique" and
"sterling" and "Georgian" silver were not enough to keep
prices up. For many, it turned out to be news that there had
been four Georges throned in England in antiquity—and
only the silver made during the reign of George I was still
holding its own on the market, and very nicely, too. It suddenly occurred to many people that a knowledge of history
was important to wise investment in antique silver. Com-

menting on the sudden shake-up in prices, an executive in one of the nation's largest auction houses put it this way:

"It was never really a stable market. With all the rush to invest in silver, the untutored saw only price and never understood that certain kinds of pieces never hold their own for very long. People were investing money in South American silver, Mexican, late German—which isn't even sterling—and even modern. I can understand the other kind of buying. After all, there is something very hypnotic about that word 'antique,' especially when antiques are booming. But what did anybody expect to happen to modern silver? It doesn't take any kind of high expertise to know that if you buy a new silver service for $1,000 today, you'll only get $500 if you sell it tomorrow."

What had happened in the 1960s is easy to see now—and was easy to see then. As the prices of antique silver began to climb, people holding old heirloom silver brought it out of the attic and to the auction bench. But as a look at the dictionary will show, "heirloom" does not mean authenticity, quality, rarity, or good workmanship and artistry. Modern times do not have the exclusive patent to turn out junk. Nor does antiquity hold the franchise for making perfection. And so, by and by, the poorly made and undistinguished found their real market price. And the well-made and beautiful found theirs, regardless of age and name. While average prices were falling, an exquisite French chocolate pot made in 1583 brought $47,000 at auction—up 15 percent from the price eight months earlier. And a meat-fork-and-spoon set of Danish silver, made in 1928, sold in a to-the-trade-only shop for $30, a threefold increase over its price of five years before. "Why?" said the dealer who bought it. "Because it's beautiful. I can get $50 for it in my store tomorrow. If I wait six months, I'll probably be able to get $60. That's what's so nice about the market in beautiful things. It's eternal."

There's an opposite side to the market in beautiful things, too, as skillful investors know. In a wholesale antique store recently, a particularly ugly Victorian sterling coffeepot sold for $350, up from the $125 the dealer paid for it three years ago.

"Exactly," the dealer explained. "It's particularly ugly. That makes it unique among both the beautiful and the ordinary. And for part of the market, 'unique' always means price. But that's not as easy as it sounds. In today's market you have to look long and hard to find something that's outstandingly ugly."

III

Furniture

S*OME* day Boards of Education across the country are going to see the light and make every girl take a course in elementary manual training, woodworking, and cabinet-making. Of all the furnishings, art, and decoration she will buy for her home, the most expensive and most visible will be her furniture. And it is also the most difficult to invest in wisely without some basic education.

That means real education, not just experience.

"Furniture is bought twice in a lifetime," says a wholesaler who has made several million dollars. "It is bought first when the young couple is married. And it is bought again when the children are grown. But the couple, now older and wiser about everything else, don't know any more about buying furniture the second time around."

For an increasing number of middle-class Americans, the way out of this difficulty is to consult with interior decorators who, for a fee, will exercise their expert knowledge about both quality and the places to get it. But, says the sales chief of a thriving high-priced furniture manufacturing firm: "A lot of people go to decorators because decorators are supposed to know about furniture quality and construction. Well, from what we've seen in our showrooms, maybe one percent knows.

"Don't get me wrong. We couldn't make the money we're making without the decorator business. It's just that I don't know where their expertise is."

The plain fact is that furniture is a blind article, as any qualified member of that industry will tell you. "There is simply no set of rules for a consumer to follow when he comes into this market," says a spokesman for the furniture division of Sears Roebuck.

Overstuffing, veneer, and upholstery can hide a multitude of sins of workmanship. Poor quality of components, glue, and fasteners are not readily visible to the uneducated eye. Few furniture manufacturers advertise direct to the consumer, so you can't always rely on trade names. Or on the law, either. A tag that says "solid walnut," for example, is probably telling the truth. But it doesn't have to specify how thick the walnut is. There are also documented cases of outright fraud, especially in the "antique" furniture which has been made to order by a disreputable cabinetmaker. And as for counting on help from salespeople—on checking four major department stores in one afternoon I did not find one salesman who supplied more information than was printed on the sales tag.

To add one more dimension of complication, there is also the spectrum of price range. What makes a $500 dining room table better than a $375 table? Not much, says a family that wants to save the $125.

"That's most people," says an executive of a firm making medium-priced furniture. "For most people there's an overwhelming difference between those two prices for a table. Furthermore, most people don't want to spend the energy or the time buying their furniture a piece at a time as they find what they want. Most people want to buy everything all at once.

"Now that's an awful lot of money to put out in one lump sum—even if it's bought on credit. And so, naturally, the expectations of most furniture buyers are not as high as the expectations of the people who look on buying furniture as an investment in quality, beauty, and durability."

Times appear to be changing a bit, however. Several chains of low-priced and medium-priced furniture stores are putting in trial lines of better quality furniture. As the president of one of those chains explains: "People have the money for better quality. They may not know the rules of the market, or the questions to ask about the merchandise, but they do want to be reassured that their chairs and tables and cabinets won't wobble, splinter, flake, and gape in a couple of years."

Well, what can you do to get your money's worth in your furniture investment?

The answer is quite simple. Develop an eye, know what you are looking at, know what questions to ask.

There are two requirements to be fulfilled in order to be able to do this. First, begin your hunt by looking at the high quality items, regardless of what quality you plan to buy. Buying furniture is like buying anything else if you expect it to be an investment—a matter of comparison. You can't tell what's inadequate until you know what the best is. The other requirement of investing in furniture is knowing something about the materials and workmanship that go into the making, and some of the market techniques that go into the selling. If those prerequisites seem to be too time-consuming and tedious, then read no farther. From here on, this chapter is going to talk about furniture making, finishing, and merchandising.

Plastic Furniture

Recently three windows of a large department store were filled with ornately carved tables and chests and banners that proclaimed: "Now You Can Afford the Spanish Style." But as nothing was said there or in the furniture department about the kind of wood used, there was no recourse but to ask a salesman.

"Hardwood, lady," he said. "All hardwood. Solid pine."

Obviously there was no profit in further discussion with a fellow who called pine a hardwood. But nobody else on the floor had any information on the subject. So it was necessary to inquire elsewhere—the distributor, the manufacturer, and a couple of trade associations. And from them came the information that:

➔What appeared to be hand-carved wood was actually molded plastic veneer covering a pine frame.

➔No law requires that this imitation be identified by either the tag or the salesman.

➔You can forget about trying to tell the difference by eye alone. Plastics and molding have been so well perfected that wood grain, color, feel, and hand-carving can be reproduced exactly.

➔You can still go by trade name in buying real wood —nobody can say for how long. The top-of-the-line manufacturers still don't use plastic. But about half of the industry does today, and the number seems to be growing by the minute.

Now, this is not to say that molded plastic is a poor substitute for wood in furniture. On the contrary, at its best it offers several definite advantages. For one, it is much less expensive to mold an intricate piece than to have it hand-carved. A dining room suite that costs $1,000 in wood can sell for $500 if the chair backs and buffet front are molded styrene. For another, it is faster to mold than to hand-carve. A plastic French Provincial chair back plus back legs takes 42 seconds to mold—and fits exactly with the seat and front legs. In carved wood, the job would take hundreds of times longer, and the fit would vary from part to part. Moreover, plastic is very versatile. In a day when it becomes harder and harder to find walnut, oak, and cherry, the polymer chemistry laboratory can come up with a better-than-reasonable facsimile. With the cost of hand-carving prohibitive for most households, molding not only can produce copies of the finest old cabinetwork, but it can also come up with new intricate styles and designs. In addition, plastic is denser than wood, so it is harder to scratch. And being a synthetic, it can be washed with soap and water, and used in all climates and weathers without the hazards of mildew, rot, or warping.

That is at its best.

At its worst, it is a misrepresentation and an inferior material that will crack, chip, sag in the heat, turn brittle in the cold, wear down with use.

The problem is that there are all kinds of plastics and all kinds of molding methods, some of them far inferior to others. Knowing that, however, is not very helpful to the consumer who is about to spend $750 for a dining room suite. If he doesn't realize that it's plastic in the first place, he can't begin to ask the right questions.

But retailers and furniture manufacturers have been very reluctant to advertise their use of plastics as components or entire pieces. "The industry knows that the public is prejudiced against the word 'plastics,'" says a spokesman for

Shell, a major producer of the raw material. "Nobody wants to tempt that consumer resistance."

An executive with a manufacturers' association adds: "Most salesmen in furniture stores and departments that I've talked to either don't know or don't care about what they're selling. Of those who do, quite a few tell me that they won't jeopardize a sale by admitting to the customer that he's buying a plastic chair or table top."

And with simulated wood grains selling very nicely, there is no incentive for anybody to volunteer the truth. "What's the big deal," one salesman said to this reporter. "Maybe it is plastic. But you can't tell the difference. And it wears better than wood in the high-end merchandise . . ."

There is no arguing with that—except to say that it isn't wood, and it ought to be advertised for what it is. Good value is not the same as true value. And besides, how can you tell what's high-end merchandise and what's low-end if you don't know what the merchandise is to begin with?

On the other hand, there is a part of the furniture department that is obviously plastic, and no mistake about it. That area is usually the style that goes by the name of "Modern."

It is one of the wonders of the English language that the Modern style is now half a century old. And the big push in Modern today marks the fourth time that the style has tried to find a home in popular taste during the past 50 years. Now, a half century is certainly long enough for any furniture style to make its way. And by rights there should now be "Antique Modern" (designed by Walter Gropius in Germany in 1919) ; and "Old Modern" (introduced in the 1929 International Exposition at Barcelona); and "Secondhand Modern" (originally produced for the brave, new, post-World War II world) ; and now "Modern Modern."

It is one of the amazing features of Modern that no

matter what material it is made of, it usually ends up looking as though it were made of plastic. So if it has really been made of bent wood or real leather or honest-to-goodness pea beans, the store is probably going to shout that information. If it hasn't been made of these traditional materials, then the sales tag may not say anything—which means plastic.

As an investment in something to live with, Modern style can be a difficult matter, whether it is bought as an entire design for a room or only as an occasional piece or two to blend with more traditional furniture. Showrooms of traditional furniture in the market, for example, look like what they are, namely showrooms of traditional furniture. But the rooms displaying Modern have an entirely different look.

"That's easy to explain," a salesman says. "We set up the traditional furniture displays ourselves. But we hire decorators to set up the Modern. That's because Modern furniture depends on a total look. A haphazard arrangement can make individual pieces look wrong or downright ugly. And we're in business to sell individual pieces."

In addition, Modern has come to bespeak hard times to many, having been introduced and reintroduced in recession years. As one woman said to another in one of those newly laid-out Modern furniture departments: "It looks just like the lobby of the old Roxy theater. And you know what happened to the old Roxy . . ."

Undaunted, the furniture industry is pouring effort, advertising money, plastic, and beans into Modern Modern. For the first time, the Southern furniture market has put its traditional lines in second place and is concentrating on molded shelving, inflatable stools, bean bag chairs, and hollow foam accessories. What the industry is counting on this time around is price. "Until now," says one manufacturer's representative, "Modern has been out of reach of most people. The market has usually been very rich doctors and engineers and scientists—people who could afford the finest designs and had the household help to keep it in the state of perfection it demands. But now with advances in plastic manufacture, the items are much more durable and much less expensive."

A foam chair, for example, sells for $150; a beans-in-a-bag model for $125—a big drop from the $500 or $750 that Traditional Modern usually costs.

A few observers, too, see the design of Modern finally catching on. Says a house-and-home magazine editor: "It used to be that Modern used only materials of the first quality. There was no carving to cover up inferior wood. And only the finest leather and upholstery materials would do. But that has all changed. Nowadays the wood is plastic, the leather is plastic, and the insides are foam. And nobody objects because the eye of the beholder is accustomed to it."

On the other side of the issue—one that the buyer has to settle with himself before he spends his money—are furniture dealers and plastic manufacturers who assess customers differently. One dealer puts it this way: "Sure, the world has been waiting for Modern. Everything we talk about is efficient and trim and functional. But when it comes to where we live, the Mediterranean style or some style almost as intricate and ornate will continue to be bigger than Modern. For all our talk of efficiency and economy, we Americans like warmer-looking furniture that has a patina of age and doesn't always have to look spic and span."

Adds a plastics maker: "Everybody talks about Modern today. It's in all the magazine stories. But at the very most, Modern plastic furniture is 10 percent of the market. And that includes outdoor furniture."

What nobody talks about in the Modern or Traditional furniture world, however, is the plastic itself used in the manufacture. If any name is mentioned, it is usually only the trade name rather than the chemical. But the plain fact is, there is plastic—and there is other plastic. Some will last more than one lifetime, and others will crack just like the handles of the steak knives you buy at the dime store. Under the circumstances, some basic information is necessary in buying furniture made wholly or in part of plastic.

Now, generally speaking it is very easy to get the idea that plastic is impervious to everything—heat, cold, rain, stain, and so on and on. There is also the general impression, usually uncorrected by manufacturers' advertising, that plastic is strong as steel. And there is just enough truth in both of those statements to mislead a shopper.

In actual practice, some plastics used in furniture today will stain badly if furniture polish or other kinds of chemicals come into contact with them. Many plastics will scratch or crack if they are washed with hot water, strong detergent, or scouring powder. Many plastics will melt if they are put too close to high heat or if a hot object is put on them. Some plastics will dissolve if cleaning fluids of a certain kind are used on them. And as for strength, yes, they are frequently strong. But they are also brittle frequently. And that means a reinforcement is often used in them. That can be rubber, or glass, or in structural and weight-bearing parts, shafts of steel or wood. In that case there may be a problem with the expansion and contraction of the two different materials in temperature change. If, for example, the wood shaft reinforcement expands more rapidly than the molded plastic that surrounds it, the plastic may split or crack.

Generally speaking, too, the color and texture of molded plastic used in furniture are uniform all the way through— unlike veneer on wood, or even stained solid wood. As a result chips and bruises do not show up as clearly on plastic as on wood. But when wood is seriously damaged, it can often be repaired by filling, planing, sanding, restaining, etc. If plastic furniture is seriously damaged, however, the entire part—and sometimes the entire piece—must be replaced. On the other hand, plastic furniture can be washed with warm water and mild soap or baking soda. It can frequently take outdoor use better than wood. And with proper care, plastic furniture can look as good as new ten years after it was bought. But it will have no patina and none of the mellowness that comes to wood with age.

Those are the generalities about plastic furniture and furniture parts. The specifics must be noted as well, or an investment in furniture can turn out to be a loss. Here is a brief list of questions to ask when looking at furniture—and to have answered in no uncertain terms. It is a sort of introductory course to life in the late twentieth century, the kinds of things your grandchildren will learn in the cradle and in elementary school, the way past generations learned about walnut, pine, linen, and wool.

1. Is it plastic? Or is part of it plastic? The hang tags don't have to tell you. Instead, they often weasel around the subject with such terms as "pecan finish" or "walnut finish." So, you'll have to ask outright.

2. Is it really impervious to the things claimed for it? Or does it only have a resistant spray on it? With time, use, and washing, sprays come off.

3. Is it a thermoplastic or a thermoset? That is, will heat soften it or not?

4. What is the specific chemical name of the plastic? Don't let those names put you off. They're man-made and have absolutely no supernatural or magical properties. Listed below are some of the names you'll hear and some of their properties. But make sure you get the true chemical name and not the manufacturer's trade name.

Polystyrene. In its cheapest version, usually found in cheap toys for children. In furniture it's reinforced to be tough and rigid. But it is susceptible to certain chemicals (among them furniture polish). And it is a thermoplastic— meaning that it was formed while hot and will lose its form when heated again. Used in the modern, molded plastic look in furniture, polystyrene has a tendency to crack.

ABS. That stands for acrylonitrile-butadiene-styrene. Sorry about that. But it can't be helped. It's simply too late to think about going back to live in a log cabin among the birds, the bees, and the berries.

ABS is presently the darling of the modern look in furniture. It seems to withstand stress and does not need a coating of chemical-resistant spray. But it doesn't do well if washed with strong detergent or scouring powder. It's a thermoplastic, too, so keep it away from direct heat or hot objects. Moreover, the initial production cost is high, so it must be turned out in large quantity to justify the cost and keep the price down. That usually means mass-mass-production, with all that that implies regarding individual taste.

Polyester. Used both structurally and decoratively. And, molded to look like antique furniture, it has fooled more than one decorator and dealer. It's a thermoset—meaning that its shape was set while hot, but that heat won't make it molten again. And it has a good resistance to chemicals. But it is more brittle than either ABS or polystyrene. So, stay away from its use in spindle-back chairs and the like. And, needing reinforcement, it can be in trouble if subjected to extreme changes of temperature.

Acrylic. This one is commonly known by the trade name of "Plexiglass." Very popular. Very expensive in its clear state. Unlike polyester, acrylic is a thermoplastic. Watch out for direct heat. Structurally, it is 7 to 17 times stronger than glass. But it does scratch (although the industry says new sprays are making it scratch-resistant). And it can crack at the load point if it isn't treated kindly.

Polypropylene. This is the one that most often imitates

wood in hampers, wastebaskets, and ice buckets. In furniture, however, it's apt to be found in the discount houses in the $10 range. Usually it has a textured finish because it doesn't take a smooth finish well. It also collects dirt because it has a static charge.

Polyurethane. Another thermoplastic, frequently used for simulated wood decoration. But it still has problems for structural use. However, things happen very fast in the plastics industry, and some polyurethane is beginning to appear on the market in structural use. But it will take some time to find out how it does in actual practice.

Solid Wood

The cheapest furniture these days may not be plastic: it may be solid wood. The much revered Early American furniture was all made of solid maple, birch, pine, or cherry, but it contained very little artistry, having been made to be functional for colonial life. Today's solid, uncrafted furniture serves the same purpose for urban life. And it should save considerable money. So don't let the salesman tell you that it costs a little more because you're getting solid wood.

On the other hand, the most expensive furniture is sure to be wood. In the present market that position is held by certain eighteenth-century French and English pieces—no, not Provincial—and by a very few contemporary furniture makers. What makes the first quality is the artistry of the handwork and the attention to fine detail. Ancient, antique, and old furniture makers did not have the exclusive rights to those prerequisites, anymore than today's cabinetmakers have the patent on shoddy workmanship, although there are many people who cannot believe that. At a round table discussion in Buffalo one day, on the topic of consumers' dissatisfactions, a woman said to me:

"It's sad to realize that hardly any of the things we buy today will ever be considered fine antiques by future generations."

There is no realistic answer to that charge because nobody at any round table can foresee the future of the antique market. But it may be of some consolation to take a look backward instead. Colonial Williamsburg furniture, for example, commands top prices in the antique market today. And reproductions of it command top prices in new, finer lines. But at the time when it was not a "style" but merely the furniture made at that time and place, it was only a provincial type of cabinetwork, copied from the English pieces of the day. The taste leaders and followers of the day seldom bought it. Instead, they imported furniture made in the mother country. Today, for another example, nineteenth-century furniture brings fancy prices on the antique market. A pair of reproduction Sheraton chairs made in 1850 went at auction recently for $1,250. At about the same time the chairs were made, Charles Eastlake was writing his immensely successful "Hints on Household Taste" for Victorian England. And on the matter of chairs, he said:

"An old oaken chair or table made a century or two ago will frequently be found in excellent condition at the present day. But much of our modern furniture becomes rickety in a few years and rarely if ever survives a lifetime."

Suffice it to say that every age has its degrees of fine and not-so-fine workmanship and artistry. And investing in furniture—new, old, or antique—requires a knowledge of where to look for the indications of quality, and what to look for. To wit:

Veneer has until quite recently been under a cloud of suspicion left over from the nineteenth century, when unscrupulous manufacturers misrepresented merchandise, selling veneered pieces for solid. The glue of those days was water-soluble, and sooner or later the piece revealed itself for what it was. But much of the finest and most expensive furniture on the market today is made of plywood covered with veneer no thicker than 1/28th of an inch.

There are, however, two matters to keep in mind in this department. First, the plywood should be at least five layers thick. The more layers, the less likelihood of warping, splitting, and cracking. And second, the veneer should be free of imperfections. Just because the tag says "Rosewood" or "Burled Walnut" doesn't mean that it's the best. In veneers, one man's idea of beauty is another man's idea of imperfection. Some quality furniture houses will not use burled wood, claiming it is weaker than the unblemished and will eventually crack. Some furniture houses will not use rosewood marked with butterfly striations—the marks left by jungle vines that strangled the tree—claiming they are imperfections.

In any case, much of the price you pay should depend on how well the veneer is matched. The pattern, grain, color, and texture should appear uniform. If they don't, the price of the piece ought to reflect it.

The beauty of the grain is—or ought to be—a matter of individual taste. But it is also a factor in price and quality. The better quality lines of furniture are usually veneered with wood selected from the part of the tree closest to the stump. It seems that the farther out on the limbs the veneer comes from, the less desirable it is in high-priced, high quality work.

Core is the generic term for the furniture under the veneer, including the frame. If it's not five-ply or solid wood, it starts to fall into the pressed board variety that will flake and disintegrate with time. So, make sure you see the core,

which is usually visible on the back of the piece, or behind
the drawers or on the bottom. Scratch it with your fingernail
to find out how soft it is.

Inlay in the finest antique furniture is actually what the
name claims—individual pieces of wood, ivory, mother-of-
pearl, etc.—actually set into the core of the piece. But this is
not done anymore, the cost of labor being what it is. Almost
all inlay today is prefabricated in sheets of veneer and glued
onto the surface of the furniture.

Carving is at a premium today. The heavily worked
Mediterranean style is either all molded plastic or—if genu-
inely hand-carved—extremely high priced. Today, hand-carving is usually a machine process that follows a stencil-like
pattern. But on the higher-priced furniture a human hand
puts on the finishing touches. In the medium-priced lines the
handwork is at a minimum. The machine does what it can,
which often leaves quite a bit to be desired. A little comparison shopping, starting with the highest quality furniture,
will illustrate this difference very quickly.

Design, naturally, is another item of individual taste.
But you can protect yourself in the medium-price range furniture by staying with the simple designs. The trouble comes
when the medium-price factory gets too ambitious with
ornate design and, because money has to be saved somewhere
in the making, it may be in the construction of the piece. If
the furniture is cheaply put together, it won't hold up in
use.

Finish is another item to look at and also requires a bit
of comparison shopping to judge. No matter what you buy at
what price in new furniture, the chances are that the wood
has been kiln dried rather than aged and seasoned naturally.
This can't be helped if the market is to keep up with the
demand. But there are differences in the final finish applied
to the wood.

The best American furniture is only partly hand-finished. It is hand-rubbed, but the material used is usually applied by machine spray. Moreover, the grain is filled in to make the finishing easier. This filling gives the wood a more satiny, more mellow look. But it also prevents the wood from aging naturally and developing a patina.

Once the stain is applied, the preservative coating is put on and hand-rubbed. In high-priced furniture, that step accounts for about 25 percent of the cost. It is layer after layer of sanding and applying the preservative coat such as lacquer. In medium-priced furniture the finish is both applied and rubbed by machine. Frequently the spray contains both the stain and the preservative coating. So if anything wears off the preservative coat, the color may go with it.

Door frames, drawer tops, and frame edges will tell you whether the furniture has an exposed edge of veneer that can wear away in time, or a stain color covered by a shellac, varnish, or lacquer finish.

Fittings are more than decorative, or ought to be. They are often a good indication of the attention to detail paid by the maker. In that regard, some comparison shopping will reveal the differences in metals, fastenings, keyholes, and the like. Cheaper fittings are usually stamped, so the metal will be a lot thinner than cast metal fittings. Keyholes and hinges ought to look as though they had been installed by a brain surgeon. Two-part chests joined by metal grooves ought to behave like a solid piece, but you won't be able to tell until you've tried to move the item a few inches along the floor.

Legs are often an indication of quality, too. The crucial point is where they have been joined to the tabletop. If the marriage has been made by a peg that passes through the top and down into each leg, there may in time be a considerable wobble when the glue has dried or the wood has dried and shrunk or worn away by vibration. A better-made joining sets the leg into the table top or the understructure, and holds it there even after the glue has dried.

If it's an expansion table, there ought to be support for the middle when the table is opened to its widest. And the support ought to be a pretty sturdy affair.

Drawers are a dead giveaway to the cabinetwork. No matter what the price of the piece, they will probably be made of plywood. But they won't be put together the same way in the higher lines as they are in the lower.

Look for the place where drawer sides join the front and back. They should be dovetailed and should fit together almost perfectly, with no splinters to be seen and very little glue dripping about. Look also for differences from one dovetail to the next above and below it. If the dovetailing has been done by machine, each point of joining will be identical to its neighbors. If the joints have been handmade, you'll detect slight differences. As you go down the scale of quality, you will notice that the back of the drawer has been nailed on instead of dovetailed. At the lowest end, the front has been nailed on, too, and may come off with use.

Usually, too, the thinner the drawer sides, the better the quality. Thick drawer sides don't have to fit into the cabinet so well. And as for the runners that carry the drawer in and out, many furniture makers in all price ranges today are using center-guides—a rail down the middle that keeps the drawer bottom centered on the cabinet frame. Very fine furniture should not require this center-guide. But without it many drawers made nowadays would not close sure and true.

Overstuffed furniture, contrary to what you are likely to hear, does not mean "too much stuffing." It merely means that the frame has been upholstered all over—and that makes it the blindest item on the market. Without being able to see the wood, the construction, or even the material used for the

stuffing, you usually have to go on faith in the store or manufacturer. But there are some guidelines to follow.

First is comfort. Sit down on the chair or sofa. Come
back another time and try it again after you've tried others.
Then try it a third time on another day. But remember that
furniture comfort depends on more than the cushions. It also
depends on the springs, the webbing, and the stuffing material.

An overstuffed piece should be soft to the touch on the
arms, the back, and the top. In addition, the front edge
under the cushion should be springy. The exterior sides and
back should not feel hollow. The upholstery should continue
under the cushions. Moreover, you should look for separate
back cushions, and separate bottom cushions, that can be
turned around or over when one side begins to wear.

The welting should be narrow and cut on a bias. Wide
welting is easier to apply than narrow, and leaves more room
for sloppy workmanship. Welting cut on the bias is strongest.

As for the stuffing, the law requires that stores specify
the exact content. (For some reason, small upholstery shops
usually do not have to comply with that law.) There has not
been a substitute for the comfort of feathers-and-down
stuffing. But the next best is generally considered to be foam
rubber-and-down. For outside padding, hair is best—rubber-
ized or not. Stuffing for side chairs should be a combination
of horsehair and hog hair. It is one of the more expensive
materials, but since a side chair is used only occasionally
compared with the use made of overstuffed furniture, the
investment in stuffing may well pay off with a lifetime of
service.

Painted Reproductions of French furniture are usually
spray-painted by the mass-production manufacturers, and the
finishing touches applied by hand. Gum wood is usually used
in this style of furniture at the lower end, and beech, maple,

or birch at the higher, where all the painting, sanding, steel-
wooling, and rubbing are done by hand.

In either the low- or the high-end lines the antique look
is bestowed by hand by chipping the paint and covering the
final stage with a glaze of the desired tone and an umber of
the desired color.

There's no point whatsoever in buying this style of furniture unless you get the artistry that belongs to it. And that
artistry costs plenty.

Outdoor Furniture

One of the traditional U.S. rites of spring is the annual
trip to basement or garage for a solid round of hand-wring-
ing and moaning over the condition of the porch furniture.
What looked perfectly fine last autumn is now rusted, pitted,
frayed, warped, rotted, or cracked. And by the time it is
ready for use again, tempers will be the same way.

Part of the problem with today's porch furniture is the
name itself. For much, if not most, of the country today
there is no such thing as a porch. There is a lawn, a patio, a
pool side or a rooftop. But there is no porch. And to go on
calling the furniture for those places "porch furniture" is
just inviting trouble. It is outdoor furniture. And naturally
it deteriorates in the outdoors. Why are people surprised at
that?

Obviously they are surprised—and frequently angry—
either because they invested in indoor furniture for use outside, or else because nobody told them what to expect of the
materials in the furniture. So, here is a brief rundown on the
basic summer furniture with its built-in problems.

Rattan. The traditional porch furniture of a bygone era,
it simply will not do for lawn and patio unless it is taken
indoors each evening or in bad weather. Moreover, it should

probably not be put out until the heat of the morning has burned off the dew. Real rattan is the stem of a climbing palm, and no matter how it has been chemically treated or covered with preservative, it cannot survive direct exposure to the elements.

Whether rattan is supposed to be living room furniture is a matter of taste. Or of merchandising. Part of the rattan industry has upgraded their wares with a hand-rubbed finish and rawhide bindings. At the high end, a rattan armchair with cushioned seat and back but no springs can cost over $400. What kind of sales pitch is needed to get customers to invest that kind of money for that kind of indoor furniture?

"Oh, we don't have to bother with a sales pitch," one manufacturer says. "The decorators do that. They can't wait to get rattan into their clients' homes."

Wicker. Back in popularity after years of being old-fashioned. The name "wicker" is actually a catch-all for furniture of woven rattan core, reed, palambang, or even twisted paper on a wood frame. The real wicker is woven of willow whips on a hardwood frame, and is quite expensive. All in all, it's not the sort of thing to leave out all night—or in the living room, either.

Wrought iron. Now available with guarantees not to rust for ten years, it has been known to surprise some purchasers before the guarantee expires. But in any event, sooner or later the wrought iron will have to be painted. And don't count on getting your money's worth of paint protection unless you take off the rust first.

Aluminum. Outdoor furniture of aluminum doesn't have a rust problem. The rust—or aluminum oxide—that forms on the metal becomes a protective coating against further oxidation. But it does look like oxidation, with its dull and rough appearance. If you sandpaper that oxidation off, you remove the protective coat and new oxidation takes place.

One way out is to buy aluminum with an enamel finish. But that is more expensive and eventually will need touching up where the enamel has chipped off. So if you invest in unpainted aluminum, prepare to have a dull finish with a few facial blemishes. And if it's hollow-core frame such as bent tubing, get the thickest available, no matter how many trading stamps you have to invest. Then it will not blow about in the wind, nor wear through at the joints.

Redwood. Being wood, this will eventually warp, crack, or splinter from exposure. It is also usually too cumbersome to move indoors and out easily. But it is attractive in the eyes of people who are put off by a lawn full of metal. For these folks, the rites of spring mean sanding and refinishing with a protective coat each year.

Strapping-and-lacing. Another yearly problem in outdoor furniture. More and more, back and seat webbing are made of vinyl these days because of its all-weather durability. But contrary to advance billing, no cushion—or any material—can be left outside in all weather.

As for the webbing itself, nonwoven is far superior to the woven. But the thicker the nonwoven vinyl, the better it is. In addition, the more straps per piece of furniture, the more support overall and the less wear and tear on each thong. Before you buy, look carefully at the way the straps are laced on. By and by new strapping or lacing will be needed. And if you can't do the job yourself, you will have to send the piece out at a considerable cost. One company brags about its "secret way" of lacing the straps; it's very pleasant to look at, to be sure, but it has to be sent back to the factory for repair or relacing.

Upkeep and Refinishing

Regardless of the finish applied at the factory, new and old furniture has to be cared for at home if the investment is to be protected. For some reason, the myth has grown up that the job requires both ritual and incantation. And everyone, it seems, has his own pet fandango regarding the job.

For new furniture there is one bit of advice that may come in handy for those who practice the rites of wax. If you wax the furniture more than twice a year, you'll simply be waxing the wax. To be fair to the manufacturer and to safeguard what is probably a very sizeable outlay of money in the furniture, it's best to find out exactly how to take care of the piece from the people who made it. If that information isn't available at the store, get it from the factory, or the distributor. But get it.

For people who invest in old or antique furniture with the notion that they are going to refinish it themselves, there is a common three-step approach frequently encountered: (1) stripping off the old finish; (2) applying the new; then (3) storing the refinished piece in the attic, where no one is ever likely to see it and ask what happened—or taking it to a professional refinisher to have it redone correctly. That is not meant in the slightest to be funny. It is meant as a warning. To spell it out in greater detail:

1. Beware of impairing the market value of an old or antique piece. The more original the condition of this kind of furniture, the better its resale value. Consequently, don't fill in worm holes, Don't replace old nails, hardware, or wood. And whatever you do, don't modify the original design, even if the change would make the piece better looking or more serviceable. If you have an eye on the market, that advice holds true for secondhand pieces as well as old and antique. This morning's junk has a way of becoming this afternoon's collector's item nowadays.

2. Beware of new remedies for old ailments, such as new lacquer over old. In recently made pieces the two coats will probably marry. But what appears to be lacquer on a Victorian piece frequently turns out to be varnish, and the two finishes cannot be put together. Furthermore, what appears to be old varnish (50 or more years) is often a shellac type of finish. So, if you're stripping an old piece, try wood alcohol first.

3. Is it stain, dirt, or age that you're trying to take off? Age darkens wood. So does a hand-rubbed oil finish, which attracts and envelops dirt. And so does a poorly smoothed surface.

Once you've stripped the old finish off, make sure the bare wood is clean before putting on the new finish. Removers can do a lot of work, but not all. No matter how clean and smooth the wood appears, you'll have to wash it and sand it and steel-wool it to find out what you're dealing with.

4. To stain or not to stain depends on the type of wood and grain, especially in older pieces. They may not need it. Or if they do, a very weak pigment will suffice, and possibly a combination of two to get the hue the piece needs. In any case, you'll have to experiment a lot. Just reading about how to do it is not enough.

5. Beware of easy-to-follow directions on the cans. Says one professional refinisher: "The shellac I use tells me that it will dry in 4 hours. But I've found that 24 hours is more like it." Says another: "This can of stripper says to use very little and apply evenly with a brush. But I can't get it to work well unless I apply great big blobs." And, says the printed guarantee on a very expensive "antique-it-yourself kit":

". . . However, due to the possibility of improper application and adverse surfaces or climate conditions which are beyond our control, we will not be liable for more than the purchase price of this product . . ."

6. Beware of injury to your health. Actually, that should be number one on this list. Most of the refinishers

I've queried report that they get a considerable amount of work from people who have not worn protective clothing—including eye and nose masks—or have not worked in well-ventilated areas, the best, of course, being the out-of-doors. The results have been skin rash, bronchial congestion, and in a few cases, injury to the optic nerve.

7. *If you decide to have the work done professionally,* get references. Don't take your work to a refinisher unless you have talked with several people whom he has worked for. It's a good idea to look at some of that work, too. All of the hazards to your investment mentioned in this list can befall a professional—at least a not-very-good one. And there are many of those. A number of furniture shops I visited actually have discontinued their refinishing department services because of customer complaints.

IV

Paintings, Prints, and Sculptures

*I*N Manhattan, financial capital of the world, there are now more art galleries than bakeries. That ought to prove to the most skeptical that Americans do not live by bread alone.

If more evidence is necessary, there is plenty of it. On a recent afternoon, a major television company with stations from coast to coast merged with a titanic conglomerate in a $70 million deal. That transaction was duly reported in the business news pages. On the same day, however, a 100-year-old piece of canvas that had been covered with oil paint by French Impressionist Auguste Renoir went at auction for a little more than $1.5 million. But that transaction made front page news across the United States. The year before, a painting by Claude Monet sold for $1.4 million and provided the basis for a network TV documentary. And the year before that, a Rembrandt brought $2.3 million and made cover stories in three mass-media magazines.

Art, it appears, has become a vital part of the American

civilization. Every month, on the average, a new museum opens somewhere in the nation and is immediately thronged by classes of school children, art students, and just plain folks. Retrospective shows of living artists such as Andrew Wyeth and Pablo Picasso play to record crowds across the country. Everybody, it seems, knows what's happening in the art world and can rattle off the trends as easily as—well, pop, op, and camp.

But for all that, the American homes where you will find original oil paintings of any quality hanging on the wall are far outnumbered by those where you won't. Reproductions, yes. Prints and photos, of course. Even watercolors occasionally. But not paintings, and certainly not sculpture.

Strangely it is not cost that keeps the American householder from owning these original works of art. Many homes have elegantly wrought clocks, antique furniture, and lamps made from vases that cost much more than a painting. Paradoxically, it is the new national awareness of art that intimidates the American when it comes to investing in decoration for his own walls. But it is not a difficult paradox to unravel, as anyone knows who has ever sold paintings or lectured on art to the general consumer.

True, new museums are dotting the countryside and playing to record audiences. But if a child's communication with art is restricted to museum visits, he will find it difficult to get over the notion that paintings belong only in remote temples of culture. And the hazard is true of exposure to too much art history, such as the courses that are flourishing these days in schools, magazines, adult education, and on TV. It can be very disabling to look at too many slides and reproductions, and get caught up in the abstractions of names, dates, and schools of painting. Knowing all about the Pre-Raphaelites or the career of Leonardo da Vinci can be like learning everything about a foreign language—grammar, syntax, verb endings—except how to speak it.

But of all the reasons why paintings do not hang in the American living room, the biggest deterrent is the nonsense of the art market itself. People who have never heard of French Impressionism or Claude Monet and Auguste Renoir are not surprised in the least to find out that their paintings are now bringing millions of dollars. Rembrandt, being a familiar museum and schoolbook name, astonishes nobody by selling at over $2 million per canvas. It seems only reasonable to the man in the street that Renoir's "Le Pont des Arts, Paris," sold for $150 in 1875, $40,000 in 1933, and $1,550,000 now. On the contrary, not only it is reasonable, but everybody expects it. The general theory seems to be that if you take a canvas—any canvas—and age it for a century, the price will automatically skyrocket. And the more centuries you age it, why, the more money it will bring. The only stipulation, of course, is that the artist sign his name in the beginning, so that there can be no doubt about the authenticity of the work.

For some lucky reason, this absurd idea of investing in decoration does not extend beyond the wall and down to the floor or tabletop. End tables from coast to coast are festooned with porcelains and pottery simply because they delight the eye of the beholder. Nobody worries about whether it's a pre-Columbian ashtray, the only one like it outside of the British Museum. People will go out and buy a decorated mirror just because it pleases them, without caring in the least that if it were an original Chippendale pier glass it would bring at least $400 at auction today. Nobody buys an Oriental-style vase in hopes that it will split five-for-one in 25 years—even though eighteenth-century Chinese cups and saucers are bringing $300 on the antiques market.

But when it comes to buying an original oil painting, it

doesn't matter how profoundly or personally the artist reaches out to the beholder. For some reason, the question of "investing in art" rises up like a great stone mountain between the eye and the hand. It would be a great relief to settle this matter once and for all. But after considerable effort to do so in both lecture hall and newspaper column, I have decided that it cannot be done. The minute you have answered the basic question, another just like it pops up. However, in the hope that setting it all out in black and white will clear the landscape, here are the most commonly asked questions about investing in art, and the answers to those questions as compiled from interviews with speculators, collectors, artists, and museum people:

Q. Which painters or school of painting should I buy as a hedge against inflation?

A. If you're worried about inflation, you shouldn't be buying art. You should be buying real estate or very carefully selected common stocks.

Q. With the price of antiques—especially silver— rising so rapidly, I'd like to put some money into paintings.

A. If you're planning to speculate, the best horse in the field isn't old paintings. According to past market performance, you're better off putting your money on fine eighteenth-century French furniture, Gobelin tapestries, or certain eighteenth-century English sterling silver such as pieces made by Paul DeLamerie.

Q. I'd like to make sure I can get my money out of a painting if I decide to resell it. What awards or credentials should I look for when I select a particular painter?

A. Nobody can guarantee your investment in a painting. H. Siddons Mowbray, for example, was a big name in the art world during the late nineteenth century. His "Rose Festival" won first prize at the Columbian Exposi-

tion of 1893 and was sold for $15,000—a very big price
for those days. The painting came into the market again
last year, and went for $175.

Q. What background do I need to prepare myself for buying
a painting? Is there a good book or two to read?

A. For heaven's sake, stay away from an academic approach
to the subject. There's plenty of time for reading about
painting after you have developed an eye for the real,
immediate picture.

Q. Can I trust my own taste and judgment in selecting a
painting?

A. Of course not. But you can't trust anybody else's taste
and judgment, either. But if a painting talks to you,
you'll know it soon enough. And that's all you need to
trust to begin with.

Q. Can I trust art dealers?

A. Certainly. You can trust them to try to sell you paintings.
If you're worried about a dealer's reputation, you can
check on it by asking about him at the nearest art museum.

Q. I have a friend who is quite intimidated by art galleries
and museums. What can my friend do to overcome this
feeling?

A. It is perfectly natural to feel intimidated. The art market
has made a specialty of that dish for many years. Just
remember that galleries are in business to sell paintings.
They need you. And you're there to look at the art, not
at the stage setting. Enough gallery trotting will wear
that feeling away.

Q. What if I find a painting I like—how can I tell if I'm
making a worthwhile investment if I decide to buy . . .?

And so the discussion has come full circle. For some
reason, it is very hard to keep the distinction clear between
buying a painting and speculating in the art market. But the

plain fact is that the two enterprises have only one factor in common, namely deciding which canvas to take. And apart from that, they are entirely different transactions. For one thing, you cannot speculate in art by looking at pictures. It is impossible to see a painting clearly and respond to it when you have to keep one eye on the financial and art news. And for another, it is impossible to know whether a painting says anything to you if you are buying for capital gains. It is awfully difficult to summon any real feeling for a thing when you know it is only on loan from the commodity market. And anyway, buying the gilt-edged securities in this market— the Picassos and Rembrandts—is plainly beyond the means of most buyers, whether they are investing in beauty or speculating in canvas futures.

So, unless you have plenty of money or an iron-clad tip on what the art market will be buying and selling in the next decade, there's only one basic reason to acquire a painting: namely because you respond to it wholly. That, of course, is a matter of feeling. To find that out, there are four steps to follow. They are set out below in the words of four people who create, sell, buy, and distribute this art form that has been a meaningful part of man's life since he dwelled in caves.

1. According to Robert Rauschenberg, a world-renowned American artist represented in major museums:

"The first step in buying a painting is to start looking. Just let nature take its course. If the desire to own a canvas is in your blood, you'll know it soon enough.

"But for heaven's sake, don't start out by reading books. Otherwise you'll be carrying around secondhand information. There is something wonderful about the unique, fresh quality of the beginner with his unsophisticated involvement."

2. From Tom Nolan, head of the painting department at the Parke-Bernet Gallery, the well-known auction house:

"Buying a painting is like buying a sports car, stereo, or house. You don't rush into it.

"Talk to friends who have good paintings and learn from their experience in shopping."

3. From Klaus Virch, assistant curator of the Metropolitan Museum of Art:

"Learning about painting is like learning about anything else. If you are in the stock market, you get a good broker. In the painting market, get a good dealer. This museum will recommend reputable dealers in the New York area. Most of the nation's museums will make similar recommendations in their areas."

Adds Frank Mason, senior instructor at the Art Student's League, whose work hangs in mansions and churches in the United States and Europe:

"Start with your neighborhood or local galleries. If you find a painting you like, get in touch with the artist if possible, and visit him in his studio. Get to know him and his work."

4. And, from Campbell Wyly, formerly director of the rental department of the Museum of Modern Art:

"Any new experience is frightening. But when it comes to buying a painting, most people are so intimidated that they think they need a graduate degree in art.

"If you're going to dispel this mystique, you must do more than look at paintings. You must handle them physically. And if possible, you should hang them in your home before you make a final choice. Only when your relationship with a canvas is leisurely and relaxed do you gain mature visual perception."

It's as simple as that. But as anybody in the world of art can testify, there are many people who will not believe it. They will nod reasonably when they hear it, and may even be able to repeat it word for word afterward. But when it comes to buying a painting, a small but powerful motor starts somewhere inside and they become part of the market machinery and mystique.

"There is a certain kind of art buyer whom I have never understood," watercolor master Dong Kingman once told me. "He cannot buy a painting just because he loves it. He has to be impressed by something before he buys.

"If he's not impressed by the picture itself, then he must be impressed by the name of the artist, or by the great amount of money it costs him to own it, or by something equally beside the point."

Inasmuch as this kind of investor makes up a substantial part of the art-buying population, the market is prepared for him. And he ought to know how it works if he's going to put his money into it.

To begin with, there is the recent and very profitable business in what can best be called Art-by-the-Yard. You can recognize this operation by the large paper banners in the window of the gallery that shout: "Original Oils $5 and Up!" "Invest in Paintings Now!" "Seven Times Better Than the Stock Market!"

Inside one such gallery a saleswoman recently had the following conversation with a customer who looks remarkably like this writer. It went this way:

CUSTOMER: That's a nice painting. Who painted it?

SALESLADY: Oh, we don't keep track in the $50 paintings.

CUSTOMER: At what price do you keep track of the artist?

SALESLADY: It isn't price. We only keep track if we have more than one painting by the same person.

CUSTOMER: Well, who did all those on that wall? They all seem to have the same signature. But I can't read it.

SALESLADY: I can't read it, either, dear. But it doesn't matter because the artist doesn't live in the area. But if his

name means more to you than the painting, then you
shouldn't buy it . . .

Galleries like that—and presumably conversations like
that—are in operation in most major U.S. cities today, and a
lot of smaller ones. "And while it's not quite fraud yet," says
a member of the Attorney General's office in a state now
investigating the matter, "there is no doubt that the snake
oil industry has discovered the new American yearning for
paintings."

What keeps it from being fraud is the fact that all of the
paintings are original oils as advertised. But whether they are
art as advertised is open to question. "Much of this work
appears to be the product of a human assembly line," says a
detective from Chicago who has just returned from a European trip. "The canvases are yards long to begin with, and
are stretched across the wall of a factory or warehouse. One
workman comes along and blocks out the picture, either
with a stencil or freehand. He repeats that outline every two
or three feet. He is followed by another workman who comes
along with a can of green paint, say, and paints in all of the
trees in all of the paintings. He, in turn, is followed by another fellow with blue paint who does all of the sky down the
line. And so on until the whole canvas is filled up with paint
and the pictures are done.

"As soon as it is dry, it is rolled up, shipped to the
United States, and once through customs it is cut up into
individual paintings and sold for what the traffic will
bear."

No gallery in the art-by-the-yard business will admit to
that practice. But it's awfully hard to find out much about
the artists represented. In one gallery that sells a lot of works
of somebody named George Ferrari, the salesman identified
the artist as "an Italian painter working in Naples. We buy
every single piece of his work because he's so wonderful. But

you know how these creative people are. He doesn't want to let us release any information about him." In another, similar gallery, an inquiry about one of the artists represented was answered with a printed blurb that said only, "He was born in Amsterdam, attended art school at a very early age because his parents saw that he could paint flowers so beautifully."

Whether it is art or commerce or fraud, it is certainly booming. One chain of stores selling canvases from $5 to $75 has branches in 28 cities, with locations in neighborhoods boasting an average yearly income of more than $15,000. "Last year," says a spokesman for that company, "we sold 56,000 pictures."

What is responsible for this new kind of gold mine? In large part it is the intimidating mystique of the art world that has left many potential investors in beauty uncomfortable everywhere except in the supermarket. As a representative of one chain operation in art-by-the-yard puts it:

"People come to us for help. They are frightened of buying an original. And yet they don't want a copy or a reproduction.

"We help these people. We tell them to relax. We ask them what kinds of scenes they enjoy in real life. If they like to look at sunsets, then they should have a painting of one to look at. It's all very simple . . ."

But, says the man from the Attorney General's office, it isn't that simple at all. "One thing that's particularly not simple is what they mean by those advertising words 'original painting.' If it's mass production, they've got to say so."

It's not hard to distinguish between an original and a mass-produced painting. One giveaway is often the edge of the canvas—the part that is wrapped around the wooden form. If the picture runs from edge to edge of the canvas and finishes up on the back of the stretcher, the chances are pretty good that it's been done by the assembly line method and cut into individual pictures later. But anybody who has looked at enough paintings in museums and good galleries or artists' studios won't have much trouble telling the difference. Whether the customer cares is another matter entirely. One browser in a $5-and-up gallery remarked to her companion, "I liked the frames in the other place better."

For the easily impressed and the intimidated, there is also another aspect of the market—the reproduction that looks like a painting.

Once upon a time, if you wanted to hang a nice picture on your wall you went out and bought a copy of Van Gogh's "Sunflowers," for example, for $5, $10, or $20 depending on the size and printing quality. It didn't look like the real thing, of course. But that was beside the point. It was pretty, and it reminded you that there was a Van Gogh somewhere in reality called "Sunflowers" that had been painted by a human. The idea of trying to fool anybody with a reproduction was completely absurd. Rather, you had some beauty, or a copy of it, to put on your wall.

That was once upon a time. Several years ago, however, a new process for making reproductions was brought to the market that used not only photographs and color plates, but also a method for exact duplication of color intensity and paint thickness of the original work. The printing itself was done on materials so like the artists' that the result wasn't called a reproduction. This method goes by the name of facsimile, and it sells in limited editions from $175 to $600.

Some dealers in original paintings report hearing that facsimiles are being sold as "good investments"—especially those printed in very limited editions. But one dealer admits that he feels telling a prospective buyer that a reproduction, even a perfect one, will increase in value "is not complete nonsense. After all, a portfolio of lithographs by Degas sold for $150 in the 1920s, and it's up to $1,000 now. Of course those are reproductions made from a stone that Degas did himself. But the fact remains that they are reproductions in a limited edition. And in furniture, fine quality nineteenth-century reproductions of eighteenth-century furniture are commanding very high prices. There are many factors involved in the market for reproductions, but a market exists. And facsimiles can't be counted out of it."

The facsimile manufacturers deny the charge that their products are being sold as good investments. Says Bing Broido, vice-president of Hament Chromographics: "I don't talk about value. All I ask is, don't you think it's better to have a superb reproduction of a Cézanne than an original by an anonymous painter?"

But it is not as either a speculation nor a flawless copy of the great that the facsimile makes its greatest appeal to those intimated by the art market mystique. Only an inveterate pony player would expect to make a big killing on a $175 copy of "The Blue Boy" or "Christina's World." Despite the simulation of brush strokes, paint thickness, and color fidelity on canvaslike material, the facsimile doesn't fool even a partially educated eye—at least not in the present state of the technology. But as one art dealer points out: "A lot of completely uneducated eyes have a lot of money these days. And if they've bought a facsimile of a little-known work by a well-known name, there are certain circles where it would pass unquestioned on their living room walls as an original Klee or Pollock."

A denial of merchandising that way comes from a spokesman for the Deitz Co., a German manufacturer of facsimiles. "What many of our customers seem to want," he says, "is prestige. Our mail orders come from wealthy suburbs all over the country. Apparently these people need something of proven value, even though the original is on a museum wall somewhere."

But an employee of another facsimile company, asking that his name and his firm's be kept anonymous, says: "People are used to the term 'limited edition.' They know it means a run of a specified number, usually short. That term undoubtedly helps our sales—not just by hinting at a potential growth in value, but also by stressing the fact that there aren't too many of the pictures around.

"So, if you buy a perfect facsimile of a painting that isn't well known and hasn't been widely reproduced and distributed, you don't have to tell your friends that it's not an original. Not unless they ask specifically."

For the investor in prestige rather than in beauty, it's a pretty good bargain. But shopping for cut-rate status carries with it two pitfalls. First, be careful not to widen your circle of friends to include the sort of people who can spot the difference between an original and a copy. And second, don't get lulled into thinking that you've got an original because you can't see the word "facsimile" printed on the item. One company, now under investigation, stamps the identification only where it can be read by X-ray.

There's still another part of the market for customers who are not concerned so much with what the painting says to them as with the fact that it looks like an authentic original by an authentic painter. And that is the market in old or antique paintings whose pigments may be worn off by age or mold, whose canvas may be frayed and crumbling, and whose artistry may be poor or worse—but whose signature by the painter is clear and legible still. In the end, that is what the frightening mystique and expensive romance of the art market is all about: the painter's signature, and the older the better.

For the customer who cannot afford an authentic Constable or Homer but would like a signature of the same age, today's antique market is more than willing to oblige. Old, poor quality, poorly executed paintings of the nineteenth century that brought $5 or $10 a few years ago are now marked up to $100 or $200—if they are signed. If not, they are available at $5 or $10 still.

That leaves only one category of customer unaccounted for, to wit the householder of reasonable income who cannot begin to afford a Rembrandt but will not buy a painting unless he is assured that it will appreciate in price, or at least return his original investment when he gets tired of the canvas and wants another sports car instead. For him there is a place to buy on the art market, too.

The way to do so is listed below in ten easy-to-follow steps. They are not a joke, although there is a sad sort of humor about them. On the contrary, they set out the route followed by quite a few investors in art, working either alone or in combines.

1. Never, never buy a new or recent painting as an investment. Instead, buy a new or recent *painter*.

2. Get a painter who can assure you that his name is known to at least three people in the second-echelon of the art world—a critic for a monthly publication, for example, or the ex-wife of a big collector. These people will help circulate the painter's name when the time comes.

3. Make sure your artist has talent and personality, or flash and personality, or a new style of painting and personality.

4. His personality does not have to be terribly durable. It has to last only three years in order to secure your investment and make your profit.

5. Hire a good public relations man. For less than $1,000 per month he will get your artist's name into the society columns and semi-society guest lists.

6. For the same fee the public relations man can get your name around a bit to help your investment. ("Well-known patron of the arts . . ." or "Noted collector," etc.)

7. Purchase for your artist a one-man show at a good gallery. (A good gallery in this instance means one that has been in business more than 20 minutes and has a good money-making record. A one-man show costs about $5,000 and is quite inexpensive to bring in a winner. Especially as the same fee will also do wonders for your reputation.

8. Invite the critics to the opening of the show. Pray that they come. Pray that at least two like the paintings. Bribery won't help. Not with most U.S. critics anyway. But be very careful to serve only the most expensive canapés and best quality wine.

9. Subsidize a few friends to buy a few paintings. Nothing gets art investors to buy paintings like seeing those little stars next to canvases at a show that signify "Sold."

10. While the show is on, find someone with time and money to take your artist around to cocktail parties and teach him some manners—preferably bad manners—and the standard artist-at-party chatter ("Like man, I've got this thing for the Renaissance . . .") .

So much for the first year's investment in the art market for profit. The second year is a lot easier. You buy your artist another one-man show in another gallery. The public relations man gets him a paragraph or two in the art magazines, and three or four appearances on TV. The third year is easiest of all. Your artist has another show, a fist fight at an expensive restaurant in which two teeth are knocked out, and possibly an attempted assassination by a deranged woman.

Whether or not the wound is fatal will depend entirely on how the market looks at that time.

Prints

Hatching and raising a painter, of course, is for the very rich. And so are most forgeries and misrepresentations in paintings, involving as they do big prices and big names. These maneuvers in the art market affect very few people. But in the average-income art world of etchings, lithographs, and other prints, misinformation and outright fraud are rampant.

Just because a print is signed by the artist and numbered as one of a limited run, that is no guarantee that the artist had anything to do with the making of the print, or that the run is as limited as the advertising suggests—or even that it is limited at all. And so, an investment of as little as $25 in an "original print" can be money spent unwisely. This bargain basement art fraud is so widespread, in fact, that the Justice Departments of many states are now prosecuting cases against the print market manipulators. The art department of one mammoth chain of internationally known stores has been permanently closed, because of so many lawsuits over misrepresentation of works of art.

While much of the fraud and misrepresentation can be traced to unscrupulous dealers, it often turns out that they share the guilt with the artists themselves, or with the art studios where the prints are made—and quite often with the customer, whose misinformation about the whole matter is really a tacit agreement to the transaction. Not so long ago, for example, in the home of a woman who should know better, I saw a very nicely made reproduction of a Leonardo da Vinci drawing that dressed up the living room wall so beautifully that I said so.

"Thank you," she said, taking it down from the wall. "But it's not by anybody named Leonardo. It's by somebody named Kline. See, here's his name printed on the back . . ."

How often the name of the picture framer is taken for the name of the artist is impossible to say. But in today's big print and reproduction market, it's just one more thing to keep in mind. If you don't, the chances are that nobody else will. And while the penalties aren't terribly high, there's no reason to buy something that isn't what it's supposed to be.

The hazards of buying a reproduction instead of a painting aren't nearly as great as they are of buying a reproduction in place of an original print. Even an inexperienced eye can usually tell the difference between a piece of paper that has been printed and a canvas that has oil paint on it. But when it comes to telling the difference between an original print and reproduction of it, there's a bit of schooling required. And frequently you have to go by what the dealer says if you don't know what to look for. Consequently, the first rule in buying an original print—even if it costs only $15—is to get a bill of sale from the dealer specifying exactly what it is that you have purchased. A piece of paper like that in the print market can sometimes be worth as much or more than the work of art itself.

Beyond that, there are three basic items to know about what makes an original print original:

1. That the artist alone has created the master image on the plate, stone, or block from which the print has been made.

2. That the artist has supervised the printing process, even if he hasn't done the work himself (although usually he has).

3. That the artist has approved the finished print. Usually he signifies that by signing his name on the paper and numbering the prints as they are made.

How to tell that all of those conditions have been fulfilled means either watching the artist work, or having the dealer sign his own name to a very specific statement to that effect on the bill of sale. Otherwise you have no recourse when you want to sell, put in a claim for insurance, or cash in on a rising print market.

It is not unknown, for example, for an artist—and often a very well-celebrated artist at that—to sign blank sheets of print paper and turn them over to the print studio. The signature is real. And the print is real. But put together that way, without the artist in complete control and supervising the work, the final piece of art is a fraud. It is also not unknown for an artist who has created the original plate or stone and has signed each print to let the run extend far beyond the limited number of 75 or 100 as billed. As one gallery executive put it: "There's no way for a consumer to know how many prints were made before the plate or stone was destroyed without looking at them all. And nobody gets a chance to do that."

That is not to say that dealers are blameless in cases of print fraud. Far from it. In some instances, unscrupulous stores sell photographed and printed copies of original prints. In other cases the so-called original is a reproduction cut from an old or out-of-print magazine and passed off as part of a limited run. That term "limited run" has also been redefined in the operation of today's print market. In one typical case of this redefined limited run, the original 100 signed and numbered prints are made, and then, before the plate or stone is destroyed, another 1,000 unsigned and unnumbered are printed on lower grade paper. It's not illegal, but it is unscrupulous for a dealer to sell that second run at first-run prices. So, though not actually fraud, it is enough misrepresentation to make an investment in this kind of art a risky affair to the buyer who is not forewarned and alert.

But the sharpest redefinition of original, limited-run prints is the new term, "multiple original," which originated with the pop art school. That term, according to a spokesman for the New York Attorney General's office, means "any number less than infinity." One magazine, for example, is running a series of pictures on its pages called "original offset lithographs" limited to only 65,000. Translated into English, that means a photo of a lithograph has been made, and the photo reproduced by offset printing is limited to the run of the magazine subscription list. A similar way of expressing it could be: "original printing press line drawing limited to only a half million." And that would describe the political cartoon found in the daily newspaper.

All of this is only to say that what makes an original print original and worth investing in is the artistry that made it—from start to finish. For a brief glimpse of what that entails, here is a list of the basic kinds of printmaking methods. You don't have to try them yourself to see what kind of creativity and painstaking work go into the manufacture of an original:

Woodcuts. Made by cutting into a flat block such as wood, linoleum, plaster, chipboard, and the like. The flat surface that remains is inked and pressed on the paper. The cut-away areas, being too low for the ink to reach, remain white. Knowing how to achieve shadings, delicate effects, and perspective by cutting away instead of adding on (as the artist does in a painting) requires more than just craftsmanship. Moreover, a false cut and the block is irrevocably altered.

Engravings. Made by processing the plate in the opposite way from woodcutting. In engraving, or intaglio printing, the areas that take the ink are the grooves cut away from the flat surface. These grooves are filled with ink which the paper drinks—the deeper the groove, the more ink, the richer the final color on the paper. The higher, original flat surface is wiped clean of ink before the print is made.

Copper is usually considered the best material for an

engraving. Brass is used when fine lines are particularly desirable, and zinc when cost to the artist is a consideration. The bill of sale should specify which material the artist used.

Etchings. Made by the same principle as engraving, but in this case the artist draws his design on the metal plate with an etching needle, and the depth of the groove is made by acid. Only an etching is made by an acid bath. Engravings, drypoints, and mezzotints are made by tools that gouge out the metal plate.

Mezzotints. Made from a metal plate that has been roughened so that when inked it prints a deep, velvety black. On that surface, the artist polishes, scrapes, and burnishes the metal to produce lighter tones or pure whites. Like the woodcut, the mezzotint prints by ink from the high surfaces. The lower the surface has been made by polishing and scraping, the less ink it receives and the lighter the tone it yields.

Lithographs. Made by a process unlike the others, using a stone that holds a film of water. On this stone, the artist draws his design with greasy ink or crayon. The stone is then moistened, the water adhering only to areas where no grease has been applied. Next, the ink is applied—and it adheres only to the greasy surfaces and not to the film of water, thus printing on the paper only the artist's design.

Silk screens. Made by a process like stenciling, also called serigraphy. The sheer fabric is blocked out by glue or other impermeable substances in the areas where no design is to be printed. The ink reaches the paper only through the unblocked areas of the fabric. By making several silk screens of the same design and blocking out different areas on each, the artist can ink the same paper again and again, each time adding a different color to a previously untouched part of the paper.

In addition, there are new methods of making original

prints developed daily in artists' studios. Sometimes the original form is made of wires, bits of wood and metal, ropes, chains, or pebbles. These various materials are inked individually and pressed into specially made paper that has a spongy quality when damp. When dry, the original print is three dimensional and multi-textured. As one printmaker at the Art Student's League said: "The means of mass communications are forcing us to open all sorts of ways to be individual and original, and some of the results are very beautiful and very exciting. Technology is forcing us to find new means to be human."

When it comes to such textured, individual prints, it's not hard for the untrained eye to recognize an original, limited edition piece of art. But in the other areas—woodcuts, lithographs, engravings, and the like—the mass-printed photoengraving can sometimes pass for an original. Under the circumstances, the wise investor takes a magnifying glass when shopping for prints. A look at the print that way will reveal whether or not the print is a photoengraving by showing those tiny dots that make mass-printed pictures what they are.

In addition, looking at a lot of original prints in galleries and museums as well as in artists' studios will educate the eye rapidly. Second-rate work or prints made from tired stones and blocks will stand out and proclaim themselves for what they are. Beyond that, there are four points to remember in this market:

1. Don't buy for investment for future profit. That's the art market game for professionals—or suckers. And it's as true in prints as it is in canvases.

2. Buy only from a reputable gallery. That means getting references. And if the gallery won't abide by Rule Number 3, don't buy from it.

3. Get a bill of sale that includes not only a full descrip-

tion of the print, but also a 30-day return privilege—enough time to take the print to a museum for inspection, or your money back if it doesn't pass.

4. Don't spend any more on an original print than you can afford to lose at a charity auction.

Sculpture

It was a typical auto body repair shop—clanging, banging, hissing, and glaring with welding torches. Outside of the manager's office stood a crowd of young men and women waiting to apply for a job.

"Oh sure, it's easy enough to get help," the manager said. "But keeping them is something else. Most of these kids out there are art school graduates. All they want is a place to learn welding so they can open studios and become sculptors."

The auto body repair industry may be having headaches. But the world of sculpture has never been healthier. At a recent auction, for example, a piece by twentieth-century sculptor Giacometti brought $240,000—ten times more than it sold for in 1964. At the same time, a Degas sculpture went for $300,000. And with the news of recession on the financial pages, the art pages carried news that a casting of a Rodin piece, poured long after his death, brought a record price of $4,000.

What accounts for this revival of sculpture, now selling better than at any time since the turn of the century? How is it that there is 75 percent more sculpture being shown in galleries today than five years ago? There are three general reasons.

First, said a spokesman for one of the most important art associations in the United States: "Painting is in such a mess, with a style a minute, that even the artists can't keep pace.

The buyers have been confused for years. And so, finally, the painters are turning to sculpture—and finding it very rewarding artistically, financially, and emotionally. It's very reassuring to them to be doing something again that they understand. And if you quote me by name I'll deny I said it."

The second reason for this revival in sculpture in contemporary art is stated by many artists themselves. In the words of one who has given up painting to devote himself to sculpture:"It's solid. It speaks not only to the eye, but also to the sense of touch. That makes it very relevant to people in these days when everything is symbolic, abstract, and overly stimulating." And, added another artist who now divides his time between painting and sculpting: "It takes considerable skill and ability to sculpt a head or a figure. The content simply can't be overshadowed. If the skill and ability aren't there, the finished piece shows it for all to see. Promoters who call themselves painters can't make it in a market where artistry counts."

The third reason behind the sculpture boom, according to leading American artist Chaim Gross: "Modern architecture has been largely influenced by the sculpted form. But until recently, architects did not want their creations interfered with by actual pieces of sculpture. Today, however, that position has softened. You find sculpture in office building plazas, lobbies, and even in the offices themselves.

"Moreover," said Gross, "we are building with more glass window and less solid wall today. So there just isn't enough space for paintings anymore. The climate in architecture has a real influence on the return to sculpture."

But the flourishing sculpture market is not restricted to the rarefied atmosphere of big names and high prices, or even to original works. Reproductions of famous pieces, once sold only through museums and a few bookstores, are now distributed through card shops, stationery stores, jewelry departments, and even via mail order catalogues. Furthermore, art galleries that carried only paintings until a few years ago not only have added sculpture to their wares, but have also discovered a neat sideline in "the Friday nighter"—a sculpture-buying prospect who takes home a figure on approval to see how it looks. "But he usually takes it home on a Friday night," one dealer explained, "and he brings it back on Monday morning. Finally it dawned on all of us that we were lending sculpture for important weekend dinner parties to impress the guests. So, now we charge $15 to people who want to take a piece out on approval on Fridays."

All in all, the popularity of sculpture is something quite new in the American civilization. Until recently, taste in three-dimensional art was restricted to "figurines"—glass, porcelain, or pottery figures, usually small enough to be called knicknacks or geegaws. For some reason, when the figure was larger than that, or made of marble or bronze, it became an item of mystery that few were courageous enough to take home. No more than ten years ago one of the largest bookstores in New York introduced a line of sculpture reproductions with the remarkable sales pitch, to quote the salesman: "It's not only a perfect reproduction, but it's also completely weatherproof. You don't have to put it in your house at all. You can leave it in the backyard all year long."

Even the newly rich did not buy sculpture until very recently. Up to just a few years ago, as almost any art dealer can testify, when a man made a mint of money and looked around for a way to say so out loud, his venture into the art world was for paintings only—"and almost always for Impressionist paintings," said one dealer. "In trade language, the Impressionists are known nowadays as framed money."

Now, it is foolhardy to explain how to choose a piece of sculpture. Being movable, touchable, and viewable from all sides, it either speaks plainly to the buyer or else it says nothing. And there is no way to find out which unless you take it home on approval—without having to pay for that privilege. Don't deal with a gallery that objects or charges. Viewed in its gallery setting, under carefully staged lighting and background, the piece will probably look very different from the way you will see it in your home.

There are, however, some things about the materials, workmanship, and pedigree to keep in mind while judging the artistry in sculpture.

There are three traditional materials used in this art form—bronze, stone, and marble. Marble is seldom used nowadays, being a very exacting medium and difficult to work. Stone, which does not require as much skill to finish, especially in the polishing, is much more usual in contemporary work. Like marble, stone is sculpted by hand. But the hand doesn't necessarily have to belong to the artist whose name is on the piece. For at least a century it has been an acceptable practice for an artist to make a clay model and ship it to Italy to be carved in stone. It's not a universal practice, but it happens enough so that a wise investor must ask whose hand did the work.

Bronze, of course, is not hand-carved but rather is cast from a mold which has been made from the sculptor's original piece. Becasue the metal and process are expensive, several castings are usually made from the mold. A unique bronze—one of a kind—is quite rare. Generally, editions range from six to twelve, plus the artist's proof. In buying bronze, you should look for evidence of hand-finishing, such as chasing, filing, and patina. The difference between a hand-finished and a foundry-finished piece can be seen by an eye that has looked at a number of pieces of all prices and qualities. Furthermore, the piece should bear the artist's name, the foundry name, and the edition number. These are often found on the underside. Their presence doesn't guarantee that the piece is genuine, but it is better than nothing.

The date of a bronze casting is also very important to the value—especially the future value—of the piece. The casting should have been made during the lifetime of the sculptor. Posthumous casting, also called decorative casting, is generally removed from the original intent and feeling of the model made by the artist's hand. It is a startling experience to see the difference between a Rodin casting made during his lifetime and one made from the same model shortly after his death, and still a third casting made a generation later. The figure is unmistakably the same in each instance, but the language it speaks to the beholder grows less distinct and finally inaudible.

There are also terra cotta and plaster sculptures, and there are two words to say about them: don't bother. If they fall, they will break. And there are enough unbreakable materials available to make that choice unnecessary.

But whatever sculpture you buy, most especially if it costs more than $1,000, it is imperative to buy it from a truly reliable dealer. And even then, a wise investor will take a photograph of the piece and its markings and send them to a good museum with a request for the name of an expert who can verify the authenticity.

As for reproductions of sculpture, they are not only decorative but also meaningful if they speak to you. However, they are little more than a reminiscence of the original, being a different size and in different proportion from what the artist had in mind. In addition, some of the detail of the original will be lost in the translation. But for a first acquaintance with art that is more than one-dimensional, they are an excellent introduction. Just make sure you are not buying a reproduction when you think you are buying an original.

Nowadays most reproductions are made of polyester resin with a stone or bronze skin bonded to the surface. You can tell that material by the feel of it. Polyester does not have the same cool touch of the original, nor the metallic ring of solid bronze.

Be careful, too, about buying editions that purport to be limited but are really mass-produced. Collectors' clubs advertise these very heavily. But they are usually not numbered, so there's no way of telling how many have been cast. No matter how attractive they are, they don't command a premium price—so don't pay it.

V

Chinaglass

IT was to be a dinner party celebrating their seventh wedding anniversary. Naturally it called for their "special occasion" china. And he had just taken the first plates down from the storage cabinet when a startling thought hit her:

"You know," she said slowly, "I think I loathe this china pattern. And I think I've loathed it since the day I picked it out."

If everything goes according to schedule, by their eighth wedding anniversary they'll be using their everyday china for special occasions, and their special occasion china only when they need extra plates.

Exactly how often that story is played is impossible to say. But from what I keep hearing from consumers, retailers, and china designers, about two out of three young matrons cannot understand how they ever came to pick out their pattern. But because it cost an average of $29.95 per place setting when it was new, the only reasonable recourse has been to keep it (out of sight) and use it only in emergencies.

Why china buying works that way is quite easy to find out—as long as you promise your sources that you won't reveal their names. Almost every store buyer and manufacturer I've talked with over the years has agreed that the china market is basically a bride's market. Between 65 and 85 percent of a maker's line, depending on who he is, is aimed at girls between the ages of 19 and 21. So if you're over 24 and find that your china pattern no longer talks to you, and neither does the display in most stores, it's because the industry isn't really trying to speak your language. An executive for one of the best-known English china houses puts it this way:

"At the age of 20 the American bride is going through the very adult exercise of coordinating home furnishings. And naturally the experience terrifies her. As a result the bride stays with neutral taste—neither formal nor contemporary. You might say that we design for a rather mild market."

To calm this statistical bride's fears, much of today's china is designed in two basic neutral patterns. There is the plain white plate bordered with a simple band of gold or platinum, what the editor of one bride's magazine calls "Elegant conservatism." The other basic pattern is, in the words of a major china distributor, "The itsy-bitsy floral." That, as everybody knows, is a design of small flowers either over the entire plate or on only the outside band.

But placed in a dramatic retail setting—against velvet and under theatrical spotlights—these safe, insignificant patterns not only calm the fears of the bride, but also thrill her with the reassurance that she is in good taste. "It is only later," to quote a department store buyer, "that the bride becomes a young matron and gets over the early anxieties she had about setting up her household. Then suddenly she

wakes up to the fact that she's got a very boring set of plates
and cups and saucers. That doesn't happen nearly as often
with her silver and crystal because they are basically shapes
rather than patterns. A shape, no matter how boring, wears a
lot better than a pattern."

To save the bride from the risk of disappointment (and
keep her as a satisfied customer), some stores and china departments urge her to express her own taste, rather than the
taste she thinks is expected of her. To do that job right,
however, would require that the china manufacturers turn
out a wider selection of patterns. "But," says the china buyer
for one of the most elegant stores in the world, "to complain
to them about their lack of sophisticated designs doesn't do
much good. They really don't care about changing the line
very much because they know that their merchandise walks
out of the stores no matter what." And manufacturers queried on this point do not deny the charge. But they point out
that putting out experimental and daring lines is very costly
and would be reflected in a higher price. Each new color, for
example, requires a separate baking process. A plate can be
both sophisticated and too expensive to buy, say the makers.

But would it really be experimental and therefore expensive? According to the people who design the finer and
more costly lines of plates, cups, and saucers, almost no new
pattern is ever introduced into the market without having
been tested first on the college campus—that brave new
world across the generation gap peopled by the emancipated,
uninhibited, spontaneous adults of tomorrow. A true market
sampling of their taste ought to show the china industry how
today's bride-to-be really feels about the bland elegant conservatism and the itsy-bitsy-floral.

And it does. In the words of a spokesman for one fine
china house: "I really don't know anything about the youth
rebellion or youth culture, except what I'm told. But my

experience in test marketing our sample designs on the campuses is that young people are quite fearful of revealing their personal taste. Almost invariably they choose what is actually our top performance lines, the rather bland designs that are in keeping with the older, more traditional patterns of the past two or three decades."

There is, of course, the possibility that price is getting in the way of taste. No bride or bride-to-be, no matter how much a rebel or individualist, is going to spend $30 or $40 per place setting to express what she feels may be only a passing fancy or mood. For that, she would be much more likely to experiment with the less expensive china or pottery patterns. But a look into that division reveals that the top sellers are also the blandest. Says an American-based designer for a Japanese china company:

"I had thought originally that we would be doing some very original patterns for the American market, what with all this psychedelic and Zen Buddhist business that you read about. But not only are our popular patterns very traditional, but we also have not been able to introduce any of the truly oriental designs that are so popular at home. Judging by the differences between our market surveys and our actual sales, what the young people say they are and what they really are may be two entirely different things."

In either case, it adds up to the same thing: if your taste matures or changes when the honeymoon is over, there isn't an awful lot you can do about it without putting your original investment in the attic.

There is a way out, of course, although it's probably heresy to suggest it. (No, I'm not going to suggest that a bride buy only a few place settings to begin with. That's almost the same as commiting yourself to the investment by making a sizable down payment on it.)

A very wise way to invest in china from the outset is the

way a wise investor goes into the securities market—namely by building a diverse portfolio.

There is no law of either good taste or good manners that demands an uninterrupted pattern of china on the table. On the contrary, it can be quite pleasing to the eye and stimulating to both appetite and conversation to have your dinner plates of one pattern, your salad plates of crystal, and your dessert service of another pattern. Furthermore, it is not necessary that any of these separate patterns be of a particular age to match the others. Your dinner plates can be today's model, your desserts from yesterday, and your salads from antiquity. The only thing to remember—and only in the interests of sanity—is to keep each complete service of the same pattern. And if in time your taste should change, it is not an entire table of china that will want replacing. At least not all at one time.

Without the worry of sets and suites and a fully matched service for twelve to complicate matters, it remains only to recognize quality in order to invest wisely in china.

Actually, almost all levels of quality (including pottery and earthenware) start out as a paste of lowly clay, flint, feldspar, and other common materials. The fineness of the china depends mostly on the mixture of the paste, the temperature at which it has been fired, and the skill and artistry employed in the manufacture. One lifetime is not long enough to learn everything about this process, which has been in development since the dawn of civilization. But in buying fine china or porcelain, there are a few fundamental questions you should ask yourself:

When you hold a plate to the light, is it translucent? The more light that comes through, the harder the paste used and the higher the temperature used in the firing. These are usually the prerequisites for higher quality, durability, and resistance to scratches and stains. The most translucent china has had bone ash added to the paste, and is, of course, known as bone china. Adding bone ash has been a traditionally British process, but one American company is now doing it too. Fine bone china is not considered to be better quality than fine hard-paste porcelain; the one advantage of bone china is that it is whiter than the hard-paste variety. That is not to say both kinds are always of the best quality. There is inferior bone china and inferior hard-paste as well. But whatever the quality, if you throw either on the floor, it will break.

It is not unbreakability that has made fine bone china and its hard-paste counterpart so desirable. Their renown comes from the fact that they are fully vitrified—completely nonporous before the glaze has been applied, making them much more impermeable and much less likely to chip, crack, and craze than pottery. For that reason, using bone or hard-paste china every day is wiser than saving it for only company dinners and using the less durable pottery every day. The penalty, of course, is the high cost of replacing a fine, hard piece of china if it breaks.

When you look at a plate across the light, is the glaze dull? Yes, if it's hard-paste or bone china. No, if it's soft-paste. Contrary to what seems logical, when the glaze and colors gleam together, the quality of the china or porcelain is not at its highest. A very glassy glaze generally indicates a poorer type of product.

When you strike a plate lightly with your knuckles, does it produce a metallic ring? The harder the china, the more it sounds like a piece of metal when struck. At the other end of the scale, a piece of pottery will produce a dull clunk when struck.

When you run your fingernail across an unglazed area, does the china scratch your nail? On the bottom rim of the base there is usually an unglazed area. On hard china your nail will be scratched; but if the piece has been made of soft paste, then your fingernail will scratch into it.

If you find a chipped or broken piece, is the fracture smooth and clean like broken glass? Yes, if it's bone china or hard-paste. But if it's soft-paste, the fracture will expose a granular, rough, and soft surface like the original clay used in the making, and your fingernail can easily scratch it.

Now, that doesn't mean soft-paste is a poor substitute for the hard in every way. Quite the contrary, some of the finest and most beautiful china ever made was manufactured from soft paste. Our standards and expectations, today, however, have led us to look upon bone china and hard-paste as the epitome of quality. But that is a matter of taste largely, and it is changing. In any event, a table can be set with a combination of the two—bone china or hard-paste for the dinner plates, for example, and soft-paste china for the desserts. As has been said, the hard china is more bruise-resistant than the soft, although new methods of making earthenware chip-resistant are being developed. In that regard, it is worth noting that much of the earthenware and pottery made from unrefined clays and fired at low temperatures in prehistoric times have survived to today, while metal objects, harder and more bruise-resistant in every way, have rusted away into oblivion. That is probably sad news for yesterday's bride now surveying a set of 60 plates, cups, and saucers of the same pattern that do not seem as appealing in the cupboard as they did in the store.

There is, however, just enough breakage so that complete sets of antique or even old china seldom appear on the market. To the antique collector today, that does not seem to matter much. He appears happy to pay handsomely for a partial set if it is the right age—or even if it only seems so. A bona fide dinner plate used by George Washington, for example, sold for $1,500 ten years ago, and just went for $7,500 at auction. An antique Lowestoft dinner plate in the To-

bacco pattern brought $75 then and brings $400 now. It
costs between $100,000 and $1 million to buy some very old
Chinese export sets or Meissen Swan service today. And as a
consequence, the prices of the just-plain-old have skyrock-
eted, too. At a recent auction a set of twelve Victorian cups
and saucers with spurious marks went for $825, after having
sat in a shop for several years priced at $125. An art nouveau
cookie tray shaped like a lily pad went for $70, having
changed hands the year before for $15. And when an 1875
Spode tea set went for $1,500, even the buyer confided later:

"Well, no, it isn't really a set. The cups and saucers
aren't there. But there are twelve plates and two compotes.
So that makes it a sort of a set."

Behind this run on the old and secondhand is more
than a simple nostalgia or antique hunt. It is also an expression of dissatisfaction with today's bland patterns and sameness, and worry about what the future will find in the china
market. While there is no important difference between the
composition of today's fine china and yesterday's, there is a
definite difference in the execution of design. And a spokesman for Tiffany and Co. indicates that the prospects are for
an even bigger difference tomorrow. "The new china available today probably won't be available in five or ten years
from now," he says. "With the factories trying to meet huge
demand, they are moving toward automation in an effort to
keep the supply up and the price down."

Companies that wouldn't have dreamed of such a thing
25 years ago are today relying on stamping, stenciling, and
silk-screening to replace the decorating that used to be executed by hand. Aside from the charm of hand-painting,
which gave each plate its own personality, individual brush
strokes added a depth of color and pigment which automation cannot really duplicate. Nor can it produce a many-
colored pattern economically, because each new color requires a separate baking process. And in addition, certain

colors are available only in old china. Rich ruby, for example, is a gold-based pigment, and far too expensive to make and use except at prohibitive prices (Wedgwood's Ruby Tonquin is $250 per place setting). Disappearing, too, are hand-glazing, hand-piercing, and the process of building up a design with successive layers of paste. Naturally the hand-modelers who make the originals and the molds are no longer called on to design intricate or ornate patterns. As one of the most important china dealers in the United States sums it up:

"The workmanship of 50 and 60 years ago was geared to an aristocratic clientele. Today, the workmanship is geared to average human beings in a consumer market. It's no wonder they aren't overjoyed with it."

So, the word is: if you can pick up some old china of fine quality and a design you like—even if it's only the dinner plates or the compotes—do it even if the price is competitive with new china. You're buying workmanship, artistry, and what may soon be an extinct species. Just make sure the glaze is uniform on the surface and has no tiny pinholes in it. That it's secondhand rather than antique makes no difference. That condition will pass with time.

And for heaven's sake, don't start worrying about hallmarks. For one thing, they're not required by any laws of the past, so they may be real and then again they may not. And for another thing, it's plain foolishness to restrict your search to china marked "Limoges," for example. There's no magic in the name of that city alone. Would you buy a pair of shoes just because they were marked "Made In Brockton"?

Pottery

After years of promoting fine porcelain and bone china, the dinnerware market has rediscovered pottery. Or maybe it's just that manufacturers are catching up with real life. But whatever the immediate cause, Wedgwood has recently reissued its old line of earthenware called Queen's Ware. Rosenthal now has a set of porcelain dinnerware with earthenware soup plates. Unglazed, porous pottery casseroles are being heavily promoted as cooking utensils that will draw out the acids and bitterness of stews and chickens. And so on and on.

Behind this revival of pottery seem to be three indications of a change in our life style.

First and foremost, there is the vast trend toward informality. A few years ago pottery at a "company" dinner table was unheard of—and a mixture of pottery and porcelain would certainly have been considered poor taste. The second change that pottery bespeaks concerns plain, everyday economics. Fine china can sell for more than $250 per place setting, with average prices beginning at about $18.50. But you have to shop far and wide in the pottery department to spend more than $35 for the best stoneware place setting. The third change reflected in the pottery revival can be seen in the imaginative and creative designs available. Fine china, being much more expensive to make, is usually styled for the timid, neutral, bride-to-be taste that is not yet sure of its preferences and does not want to expose itself to criticism. But the buyer of pottery doesn't think in terms of its lasting a lifetime. So, both the manufacturer and the consumer are willing to experiment with color and design.

But lower cost and imaginative design are not excuse enough to throw money away. Getting a good buy in pottery requires some basic information as well as an understanding of the names and designations used in that department. To wit:

Strength and durability. As has been noted, pottery is heavier than china and is not translucent. So there is a temptation to think that it is stronger. But that's not true. Both will break; but with normal wear, pottery, being softer and porous, is more likely to chip and crack. So it's best to examine each piece of pottery carefully, making sure that the glaze is uniform, with no rough spots or unglazed areas on the working surface.

Standards of manufacture. There aren't any, regarding either what kinds of materials are used, or how much of them go into the making. The only way to invest wisely in pottery is to look at a lot of it, pick it up, feel it, compare one line with another. Fineness of manufacture will become apparent in short order.

As for the names to be seen in the market, the general term "pottery" stands for everything that is not fine china. In addition to the word pottery, there are others used commonly:

Ceramic. The British term for pottery.

Earthenware. A pottery made of clay and flintstone, off-white in color because of the amount of iron oxide in the material. First made in the eighteenth century, earthenware revolutionized table dishes for the middle class. Before that time, plates were often wood, pewter, or very primitive red clay.

Ironstone. A kind of earthenware, taking its name from the iron oxide in the flintstone. Some ironstone is fired at a very high temperature to make it less porous than the ordinary run of earthenware. But that is not an inviolable rule.

Stoneware. The material used usually by artists working in pottery. It's frequently found in signed pieces or in the very expensive and creatively designed tableware. It is related to earthenware, but is generally thicker, heavier, and less porous. It can take drastic changes of temperature, such as from oven to refrigerator—though why anybody wants to do that is a mystery.

Faience (pronounced *fie-ence*). It is the French word for earthenware. The word may have class, but the pottery is usually very porous and is baked and glazed in one operation. The cheap Mexican pottery that looks as though it would crumble if touched is an example of faience.

Majolica. A pottery with a tin oxide glaze, very opaque and usually highly colored. Those qualities are almost always used to cover poor quality ware. So majolica is generally found in ornaments rather than in plates.

If you didn't know better, you might think there was a sign demanding "Quiet Please." Except for the rustling of checkbooks and the pinging of fingernails on goblets, it could have been a library or dentist's waiting room. But it was simply another busy crystal department in a large store.

For some odd reason, there is practically no conversation involved in buying fine crystal compared with the transactions in almost every other consumer item. When it comes to buying silver, china, furniture, and the rest, most people have all sorts of questions to ask. But in the crystal department—well, they pick a pattern they like, look to see that it is very thin, and ping it a few times to make sure that it is real crystal before writing out a check.

That sort of buying can be very costly unless it is supplemented by a few facts. To cite a few examples:

THEORY: Crystal is a term denoting a special kind of glass that contains lead in addition to the basic elements of sand and potash. FACT: In the United States, the term crystal has come to mean almost any kind of glass for table and decorative use. If you're buying crystal, make sure it's lead crystal.

THEORY: The lead content gives the glass clarity and brilliance and eliminates the tints and hues found in cheaper glass. FACT: The amount of lead used does not have to be specified on the article. So you have to inquire. The finest crystal contains about 32 percent lead. Lead content of over 37 percent will turn the crystal black and make it very brittle.

THEORY: Lead crystal has a bell-like ring when you strike it with your fingernail. The note of the bell depends on the shape of the piece. FACT: Goblets, finger bowls, vases, and similar shapes have a bell-like ring. And so does common glass, depending on its weight and shape. But solid crystal figures such as birds, swans, or cubes only thud when you strike them.

THEORY: All lead crystal should have a few blemishes—bubbles, striations, etc.—which are the mark of true handcraftsmanship. FACT: The most expensive crystal on the market today has no blemishes, because of a very expensive baking process. Those companies who say that blemishes are a good sign in crystal are trying to duplicate the new baking process at a lower cost in an effort to get the blemishes out of their wares.

THEORY: The thinner the crystal, the more desirable it is. Eggshell-thin crystal is in the best taste possible. FACT: Europeans, on the other hand, prefer heavier crystal. There is no standard of elegance and good taste in this matter. There is only your own preference.

THEORY: Cut crystal is finer and requires much greater skill and craftsmanship than uncut crystal. FACT: Crystal that is to remain uncut takes much more time to produce because it must be as blemish-free as possible. Heavily cut crystal can hide a multitude of imperfections in the material.

So, both the cut and the uncut require special art in the manufacture, and both are available in high quality.

THEORY: As long as crystal isn't terribly thin, it is as strong as ordinary glass. FACT: Crystal must be treated with deference, no matter what its thickness. The material does not take readily to sudden changes in temperature. It also scratches easily. In that regard, plain glass is stronger.

THEORY: Colored crystal is not the same quality as the plain. FACT: Colored crystal can be as finely or as inexpertly made as the untinted. The coloring process requires expert craftsmanship and adds another step in the manufacturing process. Many stores, however, feel that it is an old-fashioned style, and consequently many manufacturers feel that it is not worth trying in today's market.

On the other hand, it is the full set of tinted crystal goblets, wine glasses, and the like that are bringing premium prices. So that raises the question of colored glassware.

Once upon a time (about three years ago), colored glassware on the dinner table meant only one thing—that the home furnishings had been bought at the ten-cent store. Good stemware, or at least stemware in good taste, was either crystal-clear or slightly smoked. And that's the way it has been since grandma was a girl. But somehow or other the good taste industry has once again managed to throw its engine into reverse. And now, suddenly, colored glass has assumed great chic and fashion. Where there used to be a dime-store water glass in garish red or medicinal blue, there is now an imported drinking goblet in magenta or azure for $2.25 and up. Where there was until very recently a deep tint to cover up the imperfections in cheap glassware, there is now a $29 decanter so thick with color that you can't appreciate how well-made it is. There is now, too, a pitch-black water goblet which the department store buyers say is very popular, although they cannot say exactly why.

How this change came about is quite difficult to document. Of course, it is part of the trend that has made color synonymous with fashion. In addition, it is a way to brighten a table that is set with standard, conservative, uninteresting china. And, not to be overlooked, it is a way to make homemakers spend money. And in that regard, says an executive at Georg Jensen, a trend-setting store, "the pricing of glassware is very difficult to define. It depends on many things, but none of them has much to do with the value of the materials."

Under the circumstances, it's a good idea to know what you're buying in colored glassware. And it's still permissible to save money in the good taste marketplace.

Handblown vs. pressed glass. Traditionally, more prestige is attached to handblown glass. And so is more money, because of the added cost of labor. In colored glass, however, it's frequently impossible to tell the difference between the handblown and the pressed. And, in fact, a new British machine process has done away with the telltale mold marks usually left on pressed glass. Moreover, many designs can be made by pressing that are impossible in handblown. One example is the cracked look (which was originally made by pouring molten glass into molds made of snow).

Color vs. colors. Generally, the hue of the glass is made from the metallic salts of such elements as copper, iron, and cobalt. But very little of these salts are needed to produce the desired color. Consequently, don't get sold a bill of goods that you have to pay more because it's not clear, white glass.

There are two exceptions to that rule. Red glass usually requires a double firing to get the color right. That extra step adds to the cost of production. And two-color glassware—a blue stem, say, with a yellow bowl—also requires extra work in production. And so does cased glass, an opaque glass which has one color on the outside and another on the inside.

The imports. Prices of colored glass from Italy and the Iron Curtain countries are cheaper than the same quality from Scandinavia. Sweden particularly has very high labor costs. In fact, it is quite likely that a goblet made of two-color or cased glass from Italy will cost less than a one-color glass made in Sweden.

And in general. The more complicated the mold required for the design, the more expensive the glass. But in almost no instance is the price a matter of the basic materials. Nearly all ordinary glass is made of sand with the addition of potash, lime, or soda—intrinsically cheap items. Whether the appearance of colored glass on the market will change the American table setting is hard to say. But most manufacturers are now committed to its production, and so are most stores. On the other hand, the national taste in dinner beverage has been changing in the past 20 years away from water and toward wine. And despite the dictates of fashion and decoration, there's simply no point in serving sparkling Burgundy or a deep, rich claret in a yellow glass.

Now, there is another item in this crystal-and-glass world that needs some attention by the wise investor. And that item is the mirror. Anybody who has wandered through this market knows that Lewis Carroll was a century too early with his book, *Through the Looking Glass.*

The modern version would not be a fantasy, of course. But it would be the next thing to it, namely a factual report of doings in decoration and antique departments of the mirror market, and the madness that is going on therein. For example, for $300 you can get a century-old mirror that measures 4 feet by 6 feet and barely reflects an image because the backing has either worn off entirely or has grayed with age. The big attraction about this mirror is that it is backed with mercury, a toxic material that has been outlawed for many years. So, if you had this valuable mirror resilvered to make it usable, it would be worth only the $50 a new one would cost.

A mirror frame? You can get a nice hand-carved frame measuring 3 feet by 4 feet for $3,500. The big attraction about this frame is that it was carved by hand a century ago. That does not make the carving better than work done a half century ago. It's just that 50 does not have the magic that 100 has. If you want the dealer to clean and restore this frame to good-as-new condition, the selling price goes up to $4,500.

For $750 you can get a Venetian mirror measuring 4 feet by 5 feet. This mirror was made last year. But there are two big attractions about Venetian mirrors. One is that the frame is a mirror, too, and is usually etched with a design or tinted a different color from the mirror it frames. The other big attraction is that the term "Venetian mirror" sounds to the untrained ear like the term "Venetian glass," those words having the distinct ring of a cash register in them.

What has happened in the antique and decoration industry is a revival of the looking glass—framed, unframed, wall-to-wall, floor-to-ceiling. And with this resurgence has come all the nonsense and mystique of any reborn fashion. In mirrors, however, it is a bit more nonsensical than in most other artifacts where handcrafting and artistry play a more important role.

Looked at head-on, a mirror is only a piece of glass backed with some sort of reflecting material. The price of a mirror depends on only three factors: the kind of glass used, the thickness of it, and the added machine work or handwork. The best glass is plate because it gives an undistorted image. Cheaper glass (called shock) ripples like window glass. The very best and least expensive plate glass measures a quarter-inch in thickness. If you spend more than $40 for a 3-by-4-foot mirror in this material, it had better have a bevel edge and/or an etched design on it. The bevel should be made by machine for uniformity of line and angle. Look closely at the border of the mirror where the beveled edge angles back from the flat plane of the mirror face. If the angle is uneven or if the line where it begins is crooked, look at another mirror. The etching, on the other hand, should be handmade for finer line and better artistry. If the etched design on the mirror is an attempt to depict leaves or flowers, say, then the more detail in the foliage the better the craftsmanship. No matter how sophisticated machinery becomes, it still cannot etch a design as intricately and meticulously as the human hand can do it.

If you spend more than $15 or $20 for the same sized mirror made of shock, it had better be the one used by Snow White's stepmother to look into the future. Shock glass, being cheaper than plate, returns an imperfect reflection marred by ripples, waves, and distortions regardless of what reflective material is applied to the back of the glass. If you want to get a good look at shock glass, take a look in your bathroom medicine-chest mirror. That glass is seldom plate.

As for telling the difference between antique mirrors backed with the now outlawed mercury and modern imitations, the untrained eye will probably have trouble. There are a couple of telltales to begin with if you're really in the market for an antique, but the first step is most certainly to get a detailed bill of sale from the dealer stating clearly the type, age, and origin of the mirror. Now, regarding the earmarks of antique mercury backing: The mirror will most likely be cloudy and gray and have tiny bright pinpoints here and there. The older the mirror, the more likely, too, that the backing will be cracked in a pattern resembling alligator skin. If the backing is exposed and you can peel off a bit of it with your fingernail, the chances are good that it is mercury. If you want to go to the expense, a sample of the backing can be tested chemically. An imitation mercury mirror being passed off as the real thing may also be gray and cloudy as you look at it; but the pinpoints are not bright and they have grayish rings around them that make the spots appear to be spreading. If a cracking of the backing has been forged (it seldom is), the pattern will probably not resemble alligator skin. And the chances are that you won't be able to peel the backing off. As for chemical testing, it's certainly advisable to have it done if it's a large and expensive antique mirror that is being offered for sale. There are so few authentic antique ones available in the large sizes that the likelihood of imitation is great.

But merely using this checklist of telltales without a careful study of the matter, with frequent inspections of mirrors available, is very hazardous. As the president of one of the largest antiques stores in the world said:

"Asking me to explain the difference between mercury glass and imitation mercury glass is like asking me to tell you how I know the difference between an antique porcelain figure and a good reproduction of it. I just know the difference. That's all."

Buying a mirror frame is somewhat more complicated than buying a mirror. But this matter, too, can be reduced to a few elements once you have decided on style.

Construction. A picture frame is not necessarily a mirror frame. Glass weighs a lot more than canvas, so the frame for a mirror has to be a lot sturdier.

Hand or machine carved. Framers say that it takes a trained eye to know the difference. But it doesn't take long to train the eye. If it's hand-carved wood, you'll find imperfections. Machine carving does a much slicker job. But if it's

plastic molded to look like wood, you'll have trouble telling
the difference.

Material. There's nothing wrong with a plastic or composition frame as long as it's well made. An all-plaster frame,
usually festooned and filagreed with swirls and leaves and
perhaps a cherub or two, has a way of chipping. If the frame
has gold leaf finish, get what you pay for. Brass leaf finish is
sometimes used instead. A 2-by-4-foot frame finished in 24-
carat gold leaf costs about $175 more than the same frame
finished in brass leaf.

The second chapter of a modern version of Lewis Carroll's classic would touch on the topic of glass collecting. But
it could do no more than that. Of all the mysteries of the
human mind, the most baffling has to be the current mania
that has overtaken this hobby. Hardly a week passes without
at least a dozen queries from enthusiasts of Sandwich, Bellflower, or Bristol blue glass who simply have to find a particular piece for their collections. And each time I oblige by
looking into the glass situation, there is another vivid re-
minder that Alice got into Wonderland exactly the same
way.

Compared to glass collectors, the people who save only
old license plates and bottle caps live at the height of ration-
ality. What appeals to glass collectors defies almost every rule
of collecting anything else. To begin with, a prized item
need not necessarily be handmade. A pressed glass sugar
bowl in the Bellflower pattern which was made by the hundreds of thousands a century ago and sold then for $2 is now
bringing $850 in the collectors' market. Moreover, a worth-
while acquisition does not have to be a work of art. A nine-

teenth-century American flask which has an engraving of George Washington, the Marquis de Lafayette, or the American eagle is available for $1,000 and up. Nor does old blown glass have to bear the touch of a master craftsman to be valuable. Antique glass was seldom signed, so there is no way to tell whose hand held the pipe. But there is hardly a piece of blown Sandwich glass to be had for any price today.

To round out the picture of the glass enthusiasm, many collectors do not care at all whether an item is an antique. Premium glass bowls, pitchers, and goblets—those items given away free with boxes of soap or cereal 50 years ago—are bringing very fancy prices. A covered vegetable dish, once worth 25 Kirkman's Soap coupons, is now worth $175 in American currency on the open market. Everybody knows what has happened to the prices of old Louis Comfort Tiffany colored glass lamp shades—from $0 to as high as $6,500 in the past ten years. Old decanters are almost never to be seen anymore. And where are they? Doubtless under glass somewhere.

In glass collecting, furthermore, the prize need not even be old or secondhand. Some enthusiasts collect glass for the excellence of its color, regardless of age, origin, or type. And in some cases, it doesn't have to be particularly excellent, either. Venetian glass has its own followers who are faithful regardless of how the quality varies from fine to dreadful depending on the moment of manufacture.

One-of-a-kind is another meaningless term in glass collecting, as anyone can see in dining rooms and sun parlors filled with shelf after shelf of glass candlesticks only, or open salt cellars only, or footed goblets only. Nor is the glass collector always interested in art and beauty, as the market in old whiskey bottles and telephone insulators will show. Nor does the article have to be professionally made to bring a good price. The past decade has seen a boom in home kilns.

And today glass dishes, window panels, and ashtrays assembled from bits of colored broken bottles from cellars and garages are going for $15, $25, and $50 at handicraft shows.

But of course the glass collector does not value his hoard by its cost or resale value, as can be seen by the endless sale of department store glass ships, animals, flowers and—naturally—paperweights. Never in the history of civilizations has there been so great a transaction in paperweights. No stationery store is without a large supply on hand, and the same is true of jewelry and glassware departments as well as the antique market. At an auction recently, the auctioneer held up a foot-high crystal obelisk and told his enthusiastic audience that it would be perfect for "a paperweight collector, or as a toy for the kiddies, or as a doorstop." And with that pitch, he got the bidding up to $60.

What accounts for this revival in glass paperweights is impossible to explain. Ancient Rome had them. But there was a good reason for them then, what with the wind blowing through the open fenestra, or the pueri playing games around the tabula which usually had no drawers. For the same reasons, the paperweight has been in need throughout the intervening centuries, each adding its stamp. The eighteenth century, for example, saw invention of the millefiori—a paperweight made of little tubes of colored glass embedded in a clear glass base. The nineteenth century turned them into an advertising medium. That little snow-scene-in-glass that was so meaningful to Citizen Kane was probably a promotional give-away to sell some sort of patent medicine or perhaps a memento of a tourist attraction or resort.

Today, an original French-made paperweight of millefiori brings thousands of dollars if it is signed and dated. Even the American copies made in the last century at the glassworks at Sandwich, Massachusetts, bring hundreds of dollars. And the new ones, mass-produced and not particularly finely done, either, are imported from Italy and selling well here from $5 to $50.

Today, in the busy correspondence among glass collectors, there are several newsletters put out for paperweight collectors only. But whatever the collection is—glass elephants, bottles, candlesticks—the true value of the collection is that it is made entirely of glass. And the wise investor who recognizes that fact ought to think about saving his burned-out light bulbs. They may be worth a fortune some day. And even if they're not, he'll have the beginnings of a real nifty collection of his own.

VI

Floors and Their Coverings

AFTER more than 30 years of occupancy, the wall-to-wall carpet has been replaced as *the* way to cover the floor. In its place is the area rug. Or, in the words of a salesman advising a customer recently in the rug department of a well-known home furnishings store:

"It is now in perfectly good taste to let your parquet floors be seen. You don't have parquet floors? Then I can show you a wide selection of wall-to-wall parquet. It goes on your floor just like carpeting . . . Oh, you don't want to throw your carpeting away? That's quite all right. It's in perfectly good taste to place area rugs on top of your wall-to-wall carpet . . ."

As you can see, in this era the area rug is very flexible. Everything is in good taste. Anything goes. The only difficult part is making a selection and getting your money's worth. In some ways, buying an area rug is a lot harder than buying wall-to-wall carpet for the entire house. For one thing, carpeting is usually one solid color. For another, the pile is usually plain velvet. And if you bought your carpet ten or more years ago, the chances are the fiber was probably wool. Buying an area rug is not quite so simple, and requires not only more information, but also another point of view.

To begin with, the array in design and origin is so vast today that your rugs can end up growling at each other and at the rest of the furnishings. There are, among the dizzying supply in the rug department, such diverse items as florals, Rya, Greek flokati, Danish, Indian copies of the old French Aubusson, Spanish, American, Spanish style made in Denmark, American Indian, random-sheared, and on and on. In addition, there are the synthetics to contend with, such as nylon, polyester, acrylic, and olefin among the best-known generic names, and all sorts of creative trade names for them, their chemical cousins, and their combination with natural fibers. On top of all that, there are the animal hide area rugs, and, of course, the Orientals.

In that regard, the Oriental is in the very strong position of being familiar and reassuring to a shopper in the mind-bending rug department these days. The Oriental has been around for several millenia, so its style, colors, and patterns are not a novelty, even to people who have never owned one. On the other hand, several millenia is long enough for history to have conferred a very definite meaning on the term "rug merchant." If you want to understand why people pay good money to interior decorators, just spend a half hour trying to buy an Oriental rug. If you spend a full hour at it, you can also find out why interior decorators pay good money to psychiatrists. I tried this experiment recently. And it is a little embarrassing to report that it took the rug merchant only 27 minutes to sell me completely on a $600 Hamadan, talk me out of it completely, and get my solemn promise to think about buying a $1,400 Kirman. As one dealer confided:

"It's a very sweet dollar. So many people come in knowing only that they want 'an Oriental.' And once I find out what neighborhood they live in, the rest is easy."

It doesn't have to be that way. But the awful truth is that nearly everything about Oriental rugs contradicts the American tradition of buying things. The Oriental rug is handmade rather than mass-produced, so there is no consumer testing report or seal of approval to consult on the matter. The market itself is a roaring competition among domestic and imported rugs, so there is no list price to discount, no well-advertised trade names to rely on, no comparison shopping for a better deal on a particular year or model. And as an Oriental rug can last a lifetime, or even two, the secondhand one can be as expensive as or more than the new. There is also the irresistible spell cast by a traditional rug merchant, or else the indifference and minimal knowledge of a salesman who has been borrowed from another department. All in all, it is enough to drive an investor in rugs to distraction—which is as good a way as any to describe the state of the market today. But there is a way out, and that is to separate the chaos into its component parts and look at each.

Oriental Rugs

That phrase usually defines two kinds—Indian and Persian.

In general, Indian rugs are copies of old French and Chinese designs and have been made for years for the European market. Consequently, there are few real Indian designs available, and what you are buying is manufacturing craft rather than ancient heritage. That should mean that you pay less for an Indian rug than for its original counterpart, either Persian or Chinese.

Spotting the difference between an original Chinese or Persian rug and an Indian copy requires lots of looking at both the real thing and the imitation. But that is easily done by beginning with a good, reputable rug store or department and reading the labels as you look at the merchandise. As for distinguishing among the various designs—Hamadan, Kirman, Herez, etc.—that is also a simple matter of looking. Each name means a distinctive pattern and color combination. Except for minor differences between them, one Sarouk looks like another—just as one bolt of gray flannel resembles another. The differences are in the quality of yarn, weave, and color brilliance. If you're uncomfortable about starting out in the Oriental rug market without any background, there are several excellent books available in the library, with pictures of patterns and colors. But you'll be able to spot the differences among patterns and between originals and imitations after you've shopped a bit.

In buying Indian rugs, keep your eyes open for clear color and soft wool. If the colors are muddy and the wool feels shoddy, stay away. For $300 to $400, you should be able to get an Indian copy of either Chinese or Persian 9-by-12-foot design with sharply defined color and a good hand. The durability of the Indian is another matter. Some hold their color and do not mat for years; others do not wear well. So you'll have to take a good look at the construction of the rug. That matter is treated farther along.

In the Persian-made rug department, there are a few additional cautions. First, don't listen to talk about the resale value of the rug. You can't resell a new Persian for what you paid for it, no matter how fine the craft or design. Only the dealer can get that price—unless you can make a private sale to an individual who wants your rug. And second, beware of buying Persian rugs at auction. Generally speaking, dealers get whatever is worthwhile at auction, and they know what is worth bidding on and leave the rest to the general public. In that regard, it is important to recognize that there are both reputable and disreputable auction houses in the rug market. It is not uncommon for a fly-by-night concern to rent an elegant suite in a fine hotel for a rug auction. Beware of that kind of setting. There's a good chance that the stock for sale is heavily weighted with second-rate merchandise. Unless your eye is sufficiently educated to see even color and smoothness of nap, you may not be able to spot the shoddy in the short time available before the sale begins. If you are a determined auction buyer, then make sure the auction house has been in business a while.

There's nothing wrong with buying an old or even a secondhand Oriental rug. In fact, there may be some advantages. For example, an Oriental 60 to 100 years old might well have been made as a gift, as part of a bride's dowry, or for use by the rug maker himself rather than for sale. If so, then he wanted the colors, wool, and weaving to be perfect. In the marketplace that kind of perfection made for export and sale costs money, and plenty of it. And Oriental rugs less than half a century old were more than likely made for export and sale abroad, as were most of the rugs being brought in for sale today.

That is not to say that rugs made for export and sale were designed to be shoddy. Quite the contrary. Until quite recently, export rugs, like dowry rugs, were made by hand on looms run by master craftsmen. But with the introduction of the commercial rug industry into the Middle East, the emphasis was shifted from painstaking perfection to speed of production. So all in all, if you can find an old (60 to 100 years in age) Oriental rug, it may be of better quality and workmanship than its somewhat younger counterpart.

It was only logical, of course, that machinery should have been developed to simulate the handmade Oriental rug. And it has been. Consequently, "Oriental style" rugs today are made in the United States, Italy, Belgium—and, of all places, in Persia. There's nothing wrong with machine-made Oriental-style rugs, except that they aren't Oriental and they don't have the qualities of the handmade. By rights, they should not be sold from the same floor with the real Orientals, although they are very frequently found there. When they are, they should be properly and clearly labeled. Most stores do so, but if you have any doubts, there are a couple of telltales that give the game away. For one thing, the fringe has been applied after the rug was made (in the real Oriental, the fringe is part of the warp and woof). For another thing, the machine cannot knot the yarn the way a human hand does. So, part the pile and take a look at the knotting. If it's regular and uniform and machine-made, you'll see it.

Buying a used Persian rug from a former owner has some advantages in price, too. But it's advisable to know something about both the rug and its owner before investing that way. And the same is true about buying from a dealer. But in either case, those little rug stores that are usually "Going Out of Business" are risky places to shop. And those exquisite silk rugs that are being imported for sale in such large numbers these days are not for use on the floor. Silk rugs are very fine to the touch—a fragility that limits use to wall hanging, decorative table covering, or display under the glass of a coffee table top. Wool, not silk, is the material for use underfoot in Oriental rugs. And the price bears that out. For instance, a 3-by-5-foot silk Kashan can cost $5,000, while a 12-by-18-foot fine wool Kashan will cost only $3,500. So if you're offered a silk Oriental rug for use on the floor, don't even consider the possibility, no matter what the dealer or former owner tells you.

It should go without saying that for economy in good Oriental rugs you should buy the best quality available, not only for workmanship and color, but also for longevity. But that doesn't mean buying the best rug in the store. A fine quality of intermediate class, such as Herez, will work a lot harder for you than a poorly made Kermin. But whatever the rug or its origins, be sure you see it in your home on approval. If the store you're dealing with won't let you do that, find one that will. If it's a good Oriental rug, it will last a long, long time. And that kind of item can carry a life sentence if it doesn't please your eye and your taste.

Now, in addition to the real Persians—the Bokkara, Kirman, Saruk, Nain, etc.—and the Indian versions, there are also European and American copies on the market today, as well as Japanese. The Czech, Rumanian, and Bulgarian editions are not worth talking about. American-made machine-produced copies are fairly well constructed and can be expected to last about 30 years. But by far the best copy on the market is the Japanese—frequently advertised as Hong Kong rugs. But as the quality improves, so does the price rise. Even the Japanese haven't been able to beat that problem.

Judging the quality and construction of an Oriental rug is largely a matter of comparison, as it is in judging all beautiful things. That means looking at the best to begin with, looking at a lot of it, and then looking at the rest of the supply. As to what to look for specifically, there are three basic divisions:

The back of the rug should reveal both the weaving and the knotting. The finer the knotting, the better the rug and the longer lasting. The weave should also be close and tight. A good Oriental rug has from 300 to 500 knots per square inch. So turn the rug over and start counting.

The front of the rug differs from what we've been led to look for in floor coverings. Thickness of pile means absolutely nothing in an Oriental. What you're really looking for are good colors, fine luster, and a well-executed design. And as that is information only your eye can give you, look at lots of rugs, ask the prices, and learn what the market is before buying.

Assessing the *feel* of the wool requires some practice, too. Here, comparison shopping will also help you learn to tell the difference between fine quality wool and shoddy wool that will mat easily and wear out quickly.

Area Rugs

The standards of tight weave and good quality virgin wool can be applied to other kinds of area rugs—or could be, if they were all of woven wool. But fewer and fewer seem to meet both of those requirements: they may be neither tightly woven nor wool, but rather synthetics such as polyester, acrylic, or rayon. For quite some time now manufacturers in many areas of home furnishings have been addressing themselves to a consumer who tires easily of his daily surroundings and will take steps to change it. Which came first—this capricious householder or the product that wears out on schedule—is a matter for public debate rather than for this book. Suffice it to say that a big part of the rug marketplace has been estimating a decade as the most reasonable lifetime of the area rug. As a representative for several manufacturers put it: "Affluence is the keynote of the times. Durability is not something the American woman is concerned with. What she wants are style and fashion and a rug that will last about ten years. There's really no point in having her worry about construction or fibers."

On the other hand, store buyers and dealers in rugs point to the revival of interest in Orientals as a growing consumer reaction against poorly constructed rugs. In the words of a buyer of floor coverings for a chain of department stores: "The query we keep hearing from customers nowadays is, 'How long will it last?'"

In area rugs there appears to be room for both points of

view, at least as of this writing. So, for the investor who wants
a rug that will last and wear well, in addition to tight weave
and worsted virgin wool, there are two other points to keep
in mind. First, if the rug has a pile, make sure that it springs
back after your foot has stepped on it. If the pile just lies
there, or comes back in slow motion, look at another rug.
And second, try to find out the origin of the wool. The
heaviest grades of wool, suitable for use in a floor covering,
usually come from Scotland, New Zealand, Australia, Iraq,
Pakistan, and Argentina. The American specialty has been
sheep bred for their light, fine wool that is wonderfully
suited to clothing manufacture.

For those who want a rug that will not commit them to
a lifetime of style and design, it is necessary only to take
those qualities listed above—weave, wool, and pile—and
change the signs in front of them from plus to minus before
going out to shop. There is, in addition, one further feature
to take into account, namely tufting. The tufted rug will not
last nearly as long as the woven, and the farther apart the
tufts, the shorter the life span of the rug. Furthermore, a
tufted rug with only one backing will not last as long as a rug
with two backings. You can tell that there are two backings
by looking at an unbound sample or piece of rug. Naturally
the edge binding hides the view of the cross section.

But in either case, whether the rug is an investment in
beauty or only in fashion, it should be bought on a one-at-a-
time basis. And it should, when possible, be taken home on a
trial basis to see how it lives with the other floor coverings
and colors and textures in the room.

Synthetics

Almost everybody has some idea of the properties of
natural fibers such as wool and cotton. But modern science
has added a number of new materials that can be woven,

tufted, and sheared to make a pile. And that places a new responsibility on anybody who invests in rugs today. By the laws of the marketplace, the burden of information falls on the buyer. In textiles, especially, it is only required of the manufacturer that he properly label the contents—so many parts cotton, say, to so many parts acrylic fiber. But what do these man-made terms mean? What are their consequences in care, upkeep, and hazard? Major suppliers of the raw fiber and large weaving companies frequently turn out little pamphlets explaining all the fine qualities of these synthetics. And the salesman can often explain how to have them cleaned. But just try to find out the disadvantages! So, as a beginning only, here is a very brief list of the major man-made fibers frequently found in rugs today, along with a few of the things to know about them:

Nylon is fairly long-wearing. The colors seem to hold up. Nylon is also easily cleaned and maintains a good appearance. But it came on the market with the highest static buildup of any synthetic fiber, and with that static it collected dirt unevenly. Today nylon rugs are being billed as antistatic and antisoil, those qualities having been built into the fiber itself and not sprayed on. Less static electricity means less soil buildup. In any case, the manufacturers say that nylon today shows less soil than it did. New or old, however, nylon filament is at its best in an uncut shag rug.

Polyester in its early days showed great promise of taking over much of the synthetic market. But that bloom is off the rose, many textile people believe. No longer a novelty, polyester is no longer as highly promotable. It does have good resilience, and it holds color well. But it may be flammable. And it generally does not hold up under wear. It may be beautiful when new, but within a year or two it will probably start to look like an old rug. Also, it stains, especially by any substance with an oil base, although ink and wine come out readily.

Polypropylene still needs a lot of development before it makes the grade as a first-class rug fiber. It is a heavy bulk fiber, so it covers well. It is also high in stain resistance. The color range it spans and the colors themselves are now better than they were (originally it was mostly in dark hues), but the color retention quality is not as good as it was. Moreover, polypropylene has poor resilience and a low melting point—a scraped heel can leave a score mark on the rug. All in all, the fiber in its present state is not a good investment.

Acrylic fiber, many manufacturers say, is near the top of the list of best synthetics for rug use because it most resembles wool in feel, look, and resilience. It has good color fastness and a very low static buildup. But when new, it pills and fuzzes. It may also be flammable.

Polyester and nylon combined is out in a new fiber with the trade name "Source." The chemical company that has performed this marriage says the fiber has all the best qualities of both components. But it is still too early to report on anything about it, except to say that it sells in the luxury category—about $500 for a 7-by-7-foot rug. However, it does raise the question again of trade names, and the importance of looking beyond them for the name of the synthetic itself. What with heavy advertising and promotion, it is very easy to forget that "Dacron," for example, is only a patented name for standard polyester.

There is one further word of caution about area rugs, whether of man-made or natural fibers. Shag rugs can be flammable, and the longer the shag the easier it is to be ignited.

Hides

The animal hide has a long history of association with man's dwelling places. And the bearskin rug is still around— $1,500 and up for a polar bear of good whiteness and quality with stuffed head attached. But lately a new addition to the hide rug has been seen in the area rug department and over the arm of the door-to-door salesman: the steer hide. And its selling points are (1) that it is not a manmade fiber; (2) that in good quality it is very sturdy; and (3) compared with other natural, sturdy rugs it is not very expensive. A first-class steer hide about 5 by 7 feet sells for about $70.

A skin rug on the floor is a matter of individual taste. And if it appeals to you, there are a few things to keep in mind while shopping. First, look for a shiny, healthy looking hide. If there's white in the markings, be sure it's not a yellow white. If it's black or dark, look for uniformity of color unblemished by pale spots. Second, turn the hide over and inspect the back, looking for repair patches. They're frequently necessary because steers in the United States are usually kept fenced in, and barbed wire can be injurious. Don't buy a hide with more than two repair patches.

Third, don't get sold a bill of goods that imported hides are better than domestic, or that long-haired hide comes from a better or different steer from the one producing a short-haired hide. It all depends on when the skin was taken: in winter, steer hair is longer than it is in the summer.

The fourth caution applies not only to steer hide rugs but to all animal skins and furs. Don't get stampeded by a salesman who tells you, as one told me: "You'd better choose now. The endangered-species laws prohibit us from buying and selling any more steer hides." In truth, steers are not on the endangered-species list. If they were on the verge of becoming extinct, we would not have any beef to eat. The list may save the balance of nature, and the income of some salesmen. But it certainly makes life more expensive for the species of man that doesn't bother to find out what animals are on the list.

Flooring

With the end of the wall-to-wall carpet era, the bare wood floor is no longer something to be covered up as soon as possible. For an entirely unsuspecting public the day of the area rug has dawned, with all sorts of new problems and expenses concerning the floor itself. A floor that was put down originally to be covered up with wall-to-wall carpeting usually needs a lot of help to be made presentable. And even the older floor, left over from the prehistoric day when bare wood was acceptable, generally shows the scars of both age and carpeting.

Whatever the remedy, however, one thing is certain. It's not going to be inexpensive. And it's very likely going to be discouraging unless you know exactly what you want and what look you expect to achieve. In general, there are three ways to approach the problem. They are: the stained floor; the parquet floor; and the resilient floor. A brief introduction to each follows.

The stained floor. For older floors that show gouges, gulleys, and pathways of long use, the fastest and least expensive remedy is a machine sanding and a dark stain. If you elect that remedy, remember that a dark floor is an eye-catcher. Dust shows up magnificently, and so do baseboards that have nicks and cracks or spots. And so will the scrapes and scratches that come to a floor with daily living. In addition, a dark floor darkens the entire room and sets off upholstery and drapery fabrics as well as area rug colors to either an advantage or a disadvantage. If you have a lot of black leather upholstery or deep blue or brown colors, forget the black-stained floor. But most other colors and combinations take well to it.

Now, there are all kinds of stains available for floors,

such as oil-base, water-base, and wax-base. Whatever stain you use, find out exactly how it should be cleaned and polished without interfering with the restaining when the time comes (and it surely will with a dark floor). There's nothing more discouraging than learning that all those coats of wax will have to be washed off professionally because they won't allow a new coat of stain to get to the wood.

As to the highly visible dust, there's no help for it but constant policing with mop and vacuum cleaner. Accidental stain marks left on the baseboards can be prevented by applying masking tape first while stain is being applied, a step that should not be bypassed.

Dark stain being the eye-stopper it is, the usual plan is to stain all the floors in view the same color—living room, dining room, hall, etc. Otherwise, the broad, abrupt change in tone from room to room will tend to make the area seem a lot smaller than it really is.

The parquet floor. According to flooring dealers, parquet is having a great revival. With the development of all sorts of new plastics and synthetics, wood has once again become a mark of status. That fact, of course, adds to the price. Depending on the kind of parquet squares and their thickness, you can pay from $1 to $10 per square foot—if you buy the parquet without the installation. One dealer made no bones about it:

"We struggled for years. Wall-to-wall was the fashion. Then vinyl showed up. And because decorators could make more money on vinyl than on wood, they pushed vinyl. But in the last couple of years wood has come a long way. We have a minimum charge of $300 now—even if all you want is a parquet floor for a closet."

Parquet generally comes in two thicknesses: 3/8 of an inch and 7/8 of an inch. Most of the flooring refinishers queried, caution against the thinner because it cannot be resanded after the initial operation. (Parquet should be sanded after it is put down to make it conform to the contour of the underfloor.) It will probably not require resanding for another 25 years. But when the day comes, the floor should be able to take it.

Resilient Flooring

Under the mistaken impression that wood is too expensive and too hard to take care of, many householders are turning to resilient flooring—only to find that vinyl can cost $4 or more per square foot, depending on the quality and styling. For about 35 cents per square foot, of course, there is vinyl asbestos. For even less, there is asphalt tile. But the saving in price also reflects a lowering in quality, styling, and design. "It boils down to what people think is economy," said one highly qualified observer of the home-building industry. "So, more and more builders of condominiums and middle-class homes are leaving cement or rough pine floors and letting the owner put the finished flooring of his choice on top."

As for the "care-free" quality, sooner or later that phrase will have to be dropped from the English language. Not only in flooring, but in home appliances, decoration, clothing, building materials, fabrics—no matter what it is or what it will be used for, the merchandisers are quick to say that it will not strain, stain, muss, mar, scratch, or tarnish. If it does, then all you need is a damp cloth and . . .

Nowhere is that claim heard more distinctly than in those emporiums that sell resilient flooring. But in a spot-check of several such super stores, no salesman said a word about hard use or harsh cleaning agents. No matter what type of resilient flooring was under consideration, it appeared to be absolutely care-free, even though the experience of buyers and users contradicts that sales pitch heartily. In one case, the tile was stained by grease and never looked the same again. In another, the tile became pitted and ridged by pedestrian traffic and furniture legs. In still a third home, something— the cleaning agent or floor wax—began to disintegrate the flooring. "But of course," one unhappy customer told me, "you never think it's the fault of the flooring. It's yourself whom you blame, so you go right back to the same store and try another type or style, resting assured that it's carefree."

Manufacturers, naturally, disclaim any responsibility for the outcome. One of the largest in the resilient flooring industry "sends reams of information to our dealers. But," said a spokesman, "we don't know if they read it, or if they pass it along to the customer." An executive with another flooring company explained: "We always recommend that the consumer buy our own brand of cleaner and wax, which we tailor to each type of product we sell. We can't predict what will happen with the standard commercial detergents and waxes because the makers are always changing the formula— as anybody who watches the TV commercials knows." A third flooring maker, who also packages its own brand of cleaners and waxes, admitted that the system has built-in hazards. "If you push your own brands, you discourage the customer," a spokesman said, "because your materials can only be bought at the flooring dealer's store. For most people, that's a long way to go for soap and wax. So we don't push it, and we don't ask the dealers to push it." And the dealers don't argue. Not one of the stores visited for this report volunteered information about the makers' brands.

Well, what do you do about resilient flooring? First, you forget all about the care-free come-on. If it's a floor, it gets walked on. And that means it needs taking care of.

Second, make sure you follow the manufacturer's directions for taking care of it. So inquire about maker's brands of cleaners and waxes, and use them. It's a very convincing argument to do so if you want to get your money back from them for a floor that doesn't work well.

And third, make sure you buy the right resilient flooring for the area to be covered, and know the limitations of the material before you buy it. So be sure to tell the dealer where you are going to put the flooring. Linoleum, for instance, cannot be used on below-ground-level floors.

Resilient flooring is manufactured in two basic forms: tiles and sheets. Tiles can frequently be installed in the do-it-yourself manner, therefore saving installation costs. However, there are places where sheet flooring (up to 12 feet in width) is advisable. It is better, for example, to have sheet flooring in the kitchen and foyer, both heavily traveled areas, because there are no seams to collect dirt and—especially in the kitchen—no way for water to seep through and loosen the cement. But whether in sheet or in tile form, each type of resilient flooring has its own personality with advantages and drawbacks.

Cork. Rarely used these days, it is a very quiet and luxurious floor covering. But it scratches, changes color with age, has poor resistance to oil and other stains, and generally degrades with age.

Rubber. Also rarely used now, it is durable but does not have the variety of style and color that vinyl does.

Asphalt tile. An inexpensive covering, but it lacks in durability what it offers in economy. It is brittle, so it breaks and cracks. It stains with grease, food, oil, some waxes, and solvents. It requires a wax with a water base. Generally it costs from 20 to 35 cents per square foot installed.

Vinyl asbestos. The biggest-selling resilient flooring, it is not as resistant to scratches as solid vinyl. Nor is it as resistant to chemical stains, either. Moreover, vinyl asbestos is harder than vinyl and will not be as quiet underfoot. It comes in thicknesses ranged from 1/16 to 1/8 of an inch. For maximum durability, the 1/8 of an inch guage is best. Installed, a square foot costs from 25 to 40 cents.

Vinyl. Considered to be most durable of the resilient flooring as of this writing, it also takes color better than its competitors and is soft enough to allow for molded designs. But that softness can result in dents in the floor from heavy furniture and heels, with usually no way to get rid of them. Vinyl is more stain resistant than the other resilient flooring, but still not completely so. Black heel marks have a way of remaining. The guage of vinyl varies from .090 inches to .065 inches and even thinner. But thicker does not necessarily mean more durable, as there is filler in vinyl tiles, too. However, the thinner guages have more pure vinyl than the thicker ones. In addition, some vinyl is backed with foam vinyl in an effort to make it more comfortable. This is effective when the material is new, but don't depend on the underside comfort holding out as long as the top wearing side. Installed, vinyl ranges in price from 50 cents to $4 or more per square foot.

Nonwax flooring. A new addition to the market, this is a resilient plastic material that has a high gloss finish that requires no waxing (in fact, wax will just flake off this flooring). It also resists staining, soiling, and rubber heel marks, the advertising claims say. But it is too early to tell if this is so. It costs about $1.25 per square foot installed.

Linoleum. An old standby, it does not offer the variety of color and design that vinyl does. It cannot be used in basements or on ground-level concrete. But this covering does resist grease, although it doesn't do well in contact with lye or ammonia. Installed, the cost is between 50 and 65 cents per square foot.

But the material of the floor covering, whatever it is, depends also on the quality of the flooring beneath it for both appearance and durability. That underflooring must be clean and smooth. Frequently a layer of plywood or masonite will minimize the movement of the underfloor, preventing buckling of the resilient tile or sheet. But don't count on the store or flooring salesman to tell you that. Their purpose is to sell you resilient flooring, and then to sell you a replacement for it when it wears, stains, cracks, or peels.

In any resilient flooring, the design and color should run the depth of the material rather than on the surface only. The durability of the styling will make up for the extra cost. In addition, a textured flooring will conceal the scratches that all vinyl is subject to.

But no matter what the design, texture, or material of the flooring, it will require care. Don't let loose dirt get ground in, as it will scratch the material. Wipe up any spills immediately before they have a chance to dry. There's always the possibility that some of the flooring material will come up when the dry spot is taken off.

As has been said, use the cleaning agent and wax recommended by the manufacturer. In any case, don't use an oil base cleaner. Whatever the detergent, get it all off before applying the wax or it won't adhere properly. Don't use a strong detergent too often, especially on a floor that hasn't a wax coat, or the flooring will become cloudy. Use thin coats of polish. Thick coats never dry completely, so the floor becomes dirtier faster. Never use paint, varnish, shellac, or lacquer on a resilient floor. And always support heavy furniture on blocks of wood to prevent denting. Never move heavy furniture by sliding it, or you will scratch the flooring.

Wall Hangings

These days area rugs are frequently advertised for use as either a floor covering or a wall hanging. It's hard to say whether that started the revival in tapestries or only followed a beginning trend. But either way, the revival of this fabric popular in the Middle Ages is not terribly surprising in these days of long hair on men, cutpurses on the streets, vagabonds in the parks, and wandering troubadours with their guitars. It's a rerun in life size.

The quality of a wall hanging is again judged by the standard of weaving, yarn, dye, etc. And again, it's wisest to look at the very finest on the market in order to have that standard to follow. Whether you invest in an old or antique wall hanging is a matter for your pocketbook to decide.

Ten years ago you could buy an eighteenth-century French picture woven for wall use for $500 to $1,000. Today, those same fragile threads are up as high as $10,000, and at last look the price was still climbing. Even nineteenth-century tapestries with their scenes of sloppy sentimentality are selling for hundreds of dollars—which is hundreds of dollars more than they brought five or six years ago. And so, naturally, a number of rug manufacturers have been looking into what they hope will turn out to be a mass market in wall hangings.

There is some reason to think it may work out that way. For the past decade, speculation in paintings has become too rich a proposition for the smart money. Prices are beyond recognition now, and the profit margin is small, even for the biggest dealers. So the speculation money has been going into eighteenth-century English furniture and seventeenth-century French tapestries. A spot-check of smaller galleries appears to confirm this trend. One dealer, for example, started to show tapestries six years ago and reports that his business has doubled each year since then. Another, who joined the trend three years ago, finds that his sales in tapestries rival his sales in paintings.

In addition, art museums—which can often play a very

large part in the making of a trend if not a whole market—
have joined in the revival celebration. In the past three years
at least a dozen of the largest museums in the United States
have held large exhibitions of wall hangings. Whether it is a
consequence or a coincidence, a seventeenth-century Flemish
landscape of only medium quality tapestry work changed
hands recently for $2,500—a 400 percent return on the deal-
er's purchase. "And," the new owner said, "I expect to make
a 500 percent return on it in the next couple of years."

It would not be fair to call the revival in wall hangings
purely an invention of speculators in the market. A spokesman for the Metropolitan Museum of Art termed it a "part
of America's rediscovery of handwork in a time of molds,
stampings, and synthetics." And several decorators have
pointed out that wall hanging is a necessity in some new
apartments for keeping out the sounds of neighbors through
the paper-thin walls. "But," one dealer asked, "I can't really
believe that apartment dwellers are hanging these old 14-foot
tapestries on 9-foot walls. So if you find out what they're
doing with these things, please let me know."

Whatever the purposes of wall hangings today, the
movement seems to have begun. Furniture houses have been
using copies of ancient tapestries as accessories in their model
rooms. Rug makers are tooling up to print antique scenes on
modern fabrics. Stores report rising sales of woven wall hangings carrying designs by such artists as Picasso and Dufy, as
well as woven scenes by unknowns (a 3-by-5-foot wool petit
point costing as much as $500).

Now, none of this is to say that wall hangings are in
either good or bad taste today. It depends, as usual, on the
quality of the work. There are some beautifully printed
hangings, and some crude and sloppy woven hangings in the
marketplace. There are also some magnificent silk rugs from

Japan and Hong Kong, as well as some very dramatic American Indian work that would grace any wall.

But the antique market in tapestries is firmly in the hands of professional buyers and sellers. So don't look for many bargains there.

VII

*Other Coverings
in Your House*

THAT is not the entire catalog of floor coverings. One traditional material, considered the height of beauty for thousands of years, remains to be noted. It is discussed in the following letter from a correspondent who lives in the Los Angeles area:

"We have seen quite a few rooms with marble floors in recent home decorating magazines, and thought it would be a wonderful addition to our apartment, especially as these articles always explain how easy it is to care for marble. My husband mentioned this plan to the building superintendent, who said that we would have to get clearance from the city buildings department before we could have all that additional weight put on the floor. Luckily the apartment house flooring turned out to be strong enough to support the marble covering, although we had to slip $200 to the inspector to get the certificate signed permitting us to begin work.

"But before we could begin, we received a letter from a

lawyer representing the family who live downstairs below us.
The lawyer said that his client would sue us if we installed a
marble floor because it is very noisy when people walk on it,
and it creates a constant disturbance.

"So that is where things stand at present. And we are
left with $9,500 worth of marble that has been cut to size and
is left waiting until we can set an installation date."

Well, needless to say this is not a common problem. But
it does illustrate the role of history and social setting in shap-
ing the limits of taste. Today about half of the nation is
living in urban areas, and that percentage is increasing daily.
Each day sees the addition of new apartment houses, and
with them have come smaller living areas. At the same time,
history has brought a corrosive atmosphere—the by-product
of materials that have given us new fibers and fabrics among
other things. Nylon is a coal-tar derivative, for example.
Polyester is made from petroleum. And both are reported to
be very high in the ability to resist the destructive chemicals
that make a large part of the pollution in the air. Whether
that is progress is a matter for philosophers to decide. But
whatever it is, history has rewritten the rules for wise investment in surface coverings—napery, drapery, and upholstery.

Marble

Really, this material is much too expensive for a floor
covering. And it's too hard and cold for a vast expanse anyway, and awfully hard on the feet as well. (If you have to
have a stone floor in the living room, slate is 20 to 30 percent
cheaper. In do-it-yourself kits, it costs about $1 per square
foot.)

What marble can do as a table or chest covering, and do
very well, is to vary the texture of a room's appearance. For

that purpose it is necessary to have decoratively veined and colored marble. And the more decorative, the more expensive—which, in turn, requires more care in both the selection and the upkeep.

Color and veining are matters of individual preference. But the finish on the stone should meet a few basic standards. For one thing, the polish or gloss should be uniform with no dips, rough spots, or dull areas. That gloss is not a wax. It is the stone itself, and it should be mirror-smooth. If it's not— you can tell both by running your fingers over it and by sighting across it—then either forget the piece or pay less for it. You should also run your finger along the edge to make sure that it is smooth. If it has been chipped and repolished, you should not be paying the regular price.

Contrary to the general impression, marble does have a number of susceptibilities. But so does every other covering material. These are not drawbacks. They are the nature of the material. And regardless of the modern point of view, there is a lot more to beauty than how easy it is to clean or whether it folds flat for easy storage. In the case of marble, there are two main items to keep in mind. First, it will stain, etch, and wear when in contact with acid substances such as liquor or soda water or fruit juices. And being a soft stone, marble is susceptible to nicks and scars if it is used as a surface where things will be cut. (Where marble shines in the kitchen is as a flat top for rolling out dough.)

Upkeep is a matter of limiting the use of the marble. If you have a marble cocktail table, for example, don't serve cocktails on it unless you use coasters or mats. If food or drink spill on the surface, wash it away as soon as possible. If it remains long enough to wear through the polish, you can restore the gloss with a polishing putty made for the job. But if the stain is deep enough to feel with your fingers, don't try to polish it yourself. That is a job for a professional marble worker. As for waxing marble, you don't have to, but you can. However, don't wax white marble, as it will turn yellow.

Linen

Until about a decade ago there was a fairly simple formula for an investment in table linen. For everyday use you had several cotton tablecloths. For special occasions you had a fine double damask linen. And for extra-special, if you could afford it, you had a Madeira hand applique. All of them were white. And that was that.

But it isn't anymore. Manufacturers and stores have taught today's hostess that color is what counts. Science and the leisure-time industry have taught her that ease of care is what counts. And the youth rebellion has taught her that heirlooms are a waste of time, and nothing has to last forever. So, as of this writing, damask is out. White is also out. And, as the editor of a magazine aimed at the bridal market put it, "Today's girls may be sentimental about grandmother's gift of her old tablecloth, but they don't expect their own things to last a lifetime."

In place of durability is that modern standard of "easy-to-care-for" table linen. That has meant first a cloth that requires no ironing. But, said one department store linen buyer, "The manufacturers rushed permanent press tablecloths to the market before the process was really ready for everyday use. The first entries broke after the first washing because the permanent press process made the fibers brittle. Well, the process is better now. But I still wouldn't have the cloth on my table." And, added the owner of a linen specialty shop, "The permanent press process can't be used on fine quality fabrics. The chemical process doesn't seem to take. So manufacturers are actually cutting down on overall quality to supply the demand for an easy-to-care-for table-cloth."

How well permanent press holds up seems to depend on whom you talk to. One fabric designer in a large textile house said of his firm's tablecloths, "We're lucky that big, splashy prints are in style because the colors make it hard to tell that the cloth really does need some touching up with an iron."

But even the most wrinkle-resistant have had the built-in problem of what to do about stains. Until built-in soil release was added, there was no way to get out persistent spots because bleaching was injurious to the permanent press. Soil release, however, has done much to solve that problem. But nobody in the industry is willing to say whether the antistain ability will last the life of the cloth, inasmuch as this process hasn't been in use long enough.

Another unknown is polyester. This synthetic has been in use in tablecloths for about seven years. At first it pilled and stained, but soil release and other refinements solved those problems. Today polyester is being used in most machine-made styles of embroidery and laces. But for fine handmade embroidery, linen is still the chief fabric. And, in fact, the government of Madeira bans the use of polyester for handmade appliques.

Well, where does all of this leave the consumer? According to a spot-check of importers, buyers, and textile experts there are a few things to keep in mind if you are in the market for table linen:

To begin with, linen is still the quality fiber and fabric for table use. Cotton yarn, being twisted from shorter staple (about an inch and a half long), is not as strong as linen yarn, which is twisted from staple about two feet long. So cotton must be very closely woven to wear as well as linen. That is not to say that a linen cloth should be loosely woven.

But in any weave, no matter how many threads per square inch, the warp and filling threads should be the same size. You must look closely at the fabric to make sure they are. Moreover, the slubs should be evenly distributed throughout the fabric and not bunched up at one end.

Even if the fibers have been finely and closely woven, the cloth can still be cheaply finished. So it's wise to pay attention to the quality of workmanship. Look for hand-drawn, hemstitched hems, especially in colorful linens where the hue is sometimes used to cover cheaper finishing. A hand-drawn hem can be distinguished by two characteristics. First, there should be a line of small holes parallel to the edge of the cloth, but two or three inches above it. Second, the hem should be hand-hemstitched just beneath those holes (not at the edge). In other words, the outer edge of the cloth is two thicknesses of material two or three inches wide. Buying a finely made linen tablecloth is hardly an extravagance: 64 by 120 inches should cost about $25.

The same distinguishing characteristics of a good cloth can be found on better quality napkins as well. On both napkins and tablecloths, the corners should be mitred—another sign of careful workmanship. On poorer quality napery, the hem will be machine stitched or machine overcast, and the corner will be only corners. An overcast hem on a linen cloth is often the sign of a poorer quality and is generally the kind of workmanship that goes with permanent press linen, even though the price is higher than that of hemstitched, hand-drawn hemmed fabric. You're actually paying for the permanent press process, not for the quality of the cloth or the workmanship that has gone into it. In addition, permanent press finish gives the cloth a harsh feeling in the hand.

If you're buying a cloth with a fringe, be sure that the cloth has been stitched and finished and is a complete cloth even though a fringe is attached. On poorer quality cloths, the fringe hides an unfinished hem which will eventually fray.

If the fabric is colored, it should have a built-in soil release, and a tag should announce that fact. But the tag should also say that the material has been "vat-dyed" or "colorfast" or both.

These days the bulk of embroidery and applique is done by machine. And more machines with greater variety of stitches are being perfected all the time. But you should not pay the price of hand applique when you're getting machine work. There is, for example, a machine imitation of the hand-drawn hem. Like the hand-drawn, there are holes above the hem in this machine-made imitation; but you can see the machine stitching plainly, and the corners are not mitred—telltales that should be reflected in a lower price than a hand-drawn, hand-stitched cloth will command. Similarly, machine-made applique is readily visible on the back of the cloth. Hand applique, however, is almost as finely finished on both sides and never shows an underside with the stitches all linked together like the machine-hemming of a dress.

The finest hand embroidery is done in Madeira, on natural fibers only. The prices of Madeira appliqued cloths depend on the intricacy of the design and the number of colors used. Madeira work is not cheap: Four place mats and napkins can cost from $25 to $250. There are, however, two cheaper versions of Madeira hand applique. One comes from Hong Kong and covers the spectrum from very poor quality to a reasonably good imitation. A comparison between fine Madeira and fair Hong Kong work will reveal the difference immediately, even to the untrained eye. The other cheaper version of Madeira is not embroidery at all, but rather an acid-burning process used on polyester fabric. This cloth, with its design depending on where the acid has been applied, is generally used with a colored cloth beneath. The combination is pretty and feminine looking. The kind of feminine look, however, was described by one department executive as "the poor woman's Madeira."

It is important to say again that "ease of care" in linens does not mean "no care." Read the laundering instructions that come with the cloth, and if there aren't any, don't buy the cloth until the store gives you those instructions in writing. It's your gurantee. Remember, too, that a fabric with permanent press probably won't last as long as a cloth you have to iron. Soil release built into a cloth will withstand about 30 to 35 washings before it is exhausted. And if you're going to spend a sizable amount on a tablecloth and napkins, the general run of expert opinion is that you probably should buy a natural fiber rather than a synthetic.

Leather

Every 50 years, with clocklike regularity, the good taste industry rediscovers leather upholstery. And it being that time of century again, leather has been allowed back in the living room after an interim tour of duty on the executive swivel chair, the reception room bench, and the psychiatrist's couch.

The intervening years have seen the development of synthetic materials that look like leather—enough, in some cases, to be almost indistinguishable from the real thing by the average semitrained eye. But according to a spot check of upholsterers and furniture department managers, the revival has been in real leather and no doubt about it. The synthetics and imitations, no matter how effective, are not valued nearly as much as the genuine article. That has come as real surprise to the leather industry.

About six or seven years ago, for example, a substance called Corfam made its miraculous appearance in the synthetic leather market. It not only looked like leather, but also felt like leather, smelled like leather, and breathed like leather. Moreover, it was impervious to dirt, water, and the like. And it promised far more variety in color and design than was possible from the product produced by the steer. As an executive in the tanning industry said privately at the time of this miracle material, "We've just been dealt a blow from which we'll never recover."

For some reason, he was wrong. But why he was wrong is impossible to understand. Today an all-cotton dress is hardly to be found on store racks. It takes a lot of looking to find an upholstery fabric that isn't at least partly made of some synthetic fiber. And more than half of the nation's furniture manufacturers are now using some or all plastic in what used to be a totally natural wood industry. But leather has not been replaced as a top-of-the-line covering material. Today, Corfam is a competitor of other synthetic leatherlike coverings such as vinyl, and it seems to have reconciled itself to that arena.

In addition to *being* real, genuine leather, the revival also demands that the upholstery *look* like leather. The brightly dyed reds, greens, and whites that came into the leather market some years ago with the modern look were only incidentally leather. The real renaissance didn't start until the tanners came up with an antiqued look that gives leather the appearance of being 50 years old.

Now, leather is not for every living room. A psychiatrist's wife, for example, is just asking for trouble by having her couch upholstered that way. Nor is leather for every sitting surface. A room done mostly in leather can easily take on a reception room look. No matter how chic leather is, if the texture is everywhere it can become oppressive. Generally speaking, leather is at its best covering one piece of furniture—an easy chair, the sofa, or the love seat. But not all three.

Besides, the cost of leather furniture is high, especially the top quality, longest wearing variety. So, one leather item is usually sufficient. Consequently, it is necessary to know a little bit about leather before talking with the salesman. In this material, your sense of smell and sense of touch are not enough to get you your money's worth. You also have to know what the labels mean. And the piece must be labeled, because you can't tell by the feel or the appearance what the grade or quality of the leather is.

Leather. The tanned and finished hide of an animal. Through the miracles of technology, hides can be separated into six or seven layers (and each of them put to work) .

Top grain. The first, or outside layer. Usually the best for furniture, being soft, supple, and durable. As top grain gets older, it develops the patina usually associated with leather. (Upholstery made of other layers may not last long enough to develop that patina.) A top grain upholstered couch 7 feet long can cost $5,000 or more.

Snuffed top grain. A less-than-perfect top grain that has been corrected of flaws, imperfections, or injuries to the hide (from barbed wire, for example) by a light sandpapering.

Genuine leather. It means only that. If it implies anything, it's that it is not top grain but rather *deep buff*—the second layer under top grain. It should be cheaper than top grain, without the wearing quality.

Split. The third layer down. It is seldom used for furniture, being considerably less than durable. But with a rising demand for leather, it's hard to predict what will show up on the market.

Glove leather. This term does not indicate a layer, but

rather a thinness, a softness and a silky feeling. Because it is so thin and soft, it is really not a good buy in upholstery—even if it is top grain glove leather.

Suede. Once again on the fashion scene in furniture, it is not as long wearing as smooth leather. And the nap does come off in time. (The color used to come off, too, but a new process seems to have corrected that ailment.) There are two layers used for suede: top grain suede (the underside of the first layer) ; and deep buff suede (the top side of the second layer). Several manufacturers who were queried say that the wearing ability is the same for both, but the cost should be considerably less for the deep buff.

Imported leather. The price will usually be higher because cattle graze free of barbed wire fences. Consequently the hides don't have cuts and blemishes. (U.S. cattle are generally raised for beef. The hides are a by-product. So less care and worry are bestowed on their condition during grazing.)

A word about care of leather. Never, never use furniture polish, oil, ammonia, or abrasives to clean it. Keep it dusted. To clean it, use lukewarm water and mild soap. Rinse with clear water. Dry with a clean, soft cloth.

Upholstery Fabric

A journey through the land of upholstery fabric these days seems to be a course in contradictions. In a very large New York department store a furniture buyer explained: "People don't care about serviceability or durability of the fabric. What people want in upholstery today is 'a look.'" Meanwhile, across the city, in the executive office of a big fiber manufacturing corporation, a spokesman said: "We may not be giants in the upholstery business. But we're

enormous in reupholstery. And that's because people who
paid $1,000 for a sofa last year, see the fabric fall apart this
year, and they don't want it to happen again."

In the upholstery fabric market, cost often has very little
to do with price. As a jobber put it: "Cost depends on the
kinds of yarn used, the weave, the number of colors, and so
forth. The price, however, frequently has little to do with
that kind of quality. More often, price is set by what the
market will bear." Not so long ago, of course, hazards like
that did not exist. In those days, if you had your sofa reup-
holstered, there were three main choices. There was mohair,
which wasn't beautiful but would last forever. Or there was
heavy cotton, which would last half of a lifetime. Or, if you
could afford it, there was silk.

"Today," boasts a sales executive in a synthetic fiber
firm, "we've managed to drive much of the natural fiber out
of the marketplace. And very easily, too. We just point out to
the store how much money we're ready and willing to spend
on advertising our fabric and his place of business if he takes
our goods."

As a result of this heavy advertising spending, man-made
fiber consumption in the United States rose by 1.4 billion
pounds last year over the year before. Without such a heavy
advertising budget at its command, wool has remained at
about the same level of consumption that it was the year
before. Moreover, as a result of heavy promotion, the upholstery fabric industry claims that it has educated people in the
Eastern United States to want style—often at the expense of
durability. So far, it seems, the lesson has not been learned in
the Middle West, which is known in the trade as "nylon
territory."

Well, where does all of this leave the sofa or chair, and
the family that will be having them upholstered or reuphol-
stered? The answer is, in need of some basic information

before going out to select a fabric. The array of synthetics and combinations appears to be an overwhelming jumble, what with rayon, acetate, nylon, polyester, polypropylene, and on and on. But the situation isn't as complicated as it appears.

For one thing, the traditional natural fibers—wool, linen, cotton—have been the most popular and longest lasting upholstery materials. There is no evidence that they have lost that status. No manufacturer of synthetic fibers will claim that he makes fabrics that are better than the natural. The durability and wear of both the natural and the synthetic depend largely on the construction of the yarn and cloth. So regardless of the fiber or combination of fibers, look for a tightly twisted yarn and a tightly woven fabric.

A heavy, textured material is not necessarily a sturdy one. That heavy, bulky look can be achieved by a loosely twisted yarn and a loose weave, not a combination to insure long wearing. If the fabric is wool, make sure the weave is substantial. If it's linen, a mixture with cotton will give it finer look and feel. If it's all cotton, make sure the fiber is heavy.

Many fabrics on the upholstery market today are mixtures of fibers. Some combinations work better than others. While it is impossible to generalize about it, it's a pretty good idea to beware of mixtures of natural and synthetics. They wear differently. They take dye differently. And there's no guarantee that they will age uniformly, or that the fabric will stretch evenly with use.

Some of the most beautiful fabric today is made in combinations of synthetic and natural fibers, however. The selling point frequently is that the combination makes for a longer-wearing fabric. The fact of the matter, however, is that an upholstery fabric is only as strong as the weakest of its component threads. In other words, if the fabric is 50 percent cotton and 50 percent rayon, the cloth will last only as long as it would if it were all rayon. Fiber mixtures are usually concocted for the more varied and interesting textures they will produce, and not for their durability.

Many fabrics today are surfaced with such additions as stain-release chemicals and stamped-on textures. But both of those additions will wear out in time. And the chances are that they won't wear out evenly. So, by and by, the fabric will be left with cleaner patches and dirtier patches and a bald spot here and there. In that regard, no fabric can withstand dirt, soot, and the chemicals in polluted air indefinitely. Upholstery needs frequent vacuuming to keep the pollutants from building up inside where no cleaner will ever reach them. And regardless of how hard-wearing a fabric is, it will wear with use. So, if possible, buy upholstered furniture with detached back and seat cushions that can be turned over or around to spread the wear evenly and prolong the life of the upholstery and stuffing. If you're using silk—an extremely durable material in the right weave and weight—keep the furniture away from direct sunlight, which can rot the silk.

It's very important, regardless of what kind of fiber you use, to employ upholstery fabric for upholstery. Don't try to cut corners by using the thinner drapery fabrics instead. They simply will not stand the wear, having been designed and constructed to hang gracefully.

Now, as for the synthetic fibers, they fall into two very distinct categories: those made of wood cellulose base, such as rayon, acetate, and triacetate; and those synthesized in a test tube, such as the old workhorse nylon and the new olefin (also known as polypropylene) .

To start with the cellulose-base fibers:

Rayon. This one has been around for almost a half-century. It is probably the most versatile of all synthetic fibers in numbers of styles and appearances. It takes dyes very well. In its spun form it can be woven into large varieties of attractive styles. But as the spinning process requires the cutting of the long rayon filament into short lengths and twisting them into yarn, spun rayon is less durable and more expensive than its uncut version.

At best, rayon is not the tough, durable fiber that nylon is. However, no synthetic comes as close to behaving like a natural fiber as rayon. Like cotton, wool, and linen, it does breathe, thus preventing that feeling of being hot and sticky or cold and clammy. You can identify these fabrics by a careful reading of the labels.

Acetate and triacetate. Like rayon, these are also wood cellulose products, but they do not take the wear rayon takes. The fiber is not as absorbent as rayon, and is therefore harder to dye. Triacetate is an improvement over acetate, being able to withstand the heat of hot water and of a steam iron.

Nylon. This is usually considered the strongest material of the synthetics. But it does have certain disadvantages. For one thing, it feels smooth and slippery. For another, it has a very high sheen, and a tendency to stretch. And, without a sprayed-on coating, it is hard to clean. However, these problems are obscured and frequently unimportant when nylon is used as a velvet, especially a patterned velvet. It wears very well, and if it is a dark color, the stains are not a problem. Used untextured as an upholstery fabric with a flat finish, nylon looks and feels better if it has been mixed with cotton or another natural fiber.

Olefin. A petroleum by-product, olefin is making a big appearance on the upholstery market. It is good looking, but also very slippery—so slippery, in fact, that it often has difficulty in adhering well to stuffing and frame. To overcome this drawback, olefin usually needs a backing. Most often,

that means an acrylic spray applied to the fabric. How long
the spray will last and work is an unknown, as is the entire
question of how the olefin will look when the backing is
gone. A big improvement has been made in both the colors
that olefin will accept and in the fiber's stain resistance. This
fabric will be labeled.

Drapery Fabrics

The same standards for judging upholstery fabric can be
applied to drapery materials; but they do not have to be
applied as rigorously, inasmuch as draperies do not get the
wear, stains, or other attrition that comes to furniture. So,
the weave does not have to be as tight, nor does the yarn have
to have so hard a twist. And all in all, you can probably get
away wih a fairly inexpensive fabric that sacrifices some
durability for style.

But whatever the fabric and combination of fibers, be
sure to know the content so that you can report it to the dry
cleaner. If the fabric has a finish or sizing on it, that will
probably come out with the cleaning and the cleaner will
have to renew the finish. It's a good idea to insist that the
cleaner test the fabric before cleaning the whole drapery. He
can take material from a seam or part of a tie-back.

Draperies almost always hang better if they are lined. In
addition, the lining gives the fabric more body and also pro-
tects it from the sun and at least some of the poisons in the
air. But whether lined or not, draperies should be vacuumed
frequently to keep the pollutants in the atmosphere from
sinking into the fibers. In any event, don't use upholstery-
weight fabric for draperies. The heavier the material, the
more difficult it is to hang and pleat properly.

The fabrics used in upholstery are also found in the
drapery department, with one addition:

Glass fiber. As the name tells you, the basic fibers are made of glass in this material; therefore the fabric is highly resistant to fire. But it does have a low resistance to abrasion. You may have difficulty breaking a glass fiber by pulling it, but it will usually fall apart if you run the edge of your fingernail along it. That means gentle handling in the washing—by hand, preferably.

Whatever the kind of fabric—drapery or upholstery, natural or synthetic or combination—don't buy it unless you know what the fibers are. You can't guess at that. And you can't always believe the salesman because he may not know for sure. The only information to trust is the label, and that should be attached to the fabric.

VIII

Jewelry

THERE was a song years ago that began, "Take back your Christmas jewelry, my neck is turning green." Nobody sings that song anymore, of course, because the jewelry industry has made great strides in its look-alike division. If a chain is made to imitate gold jewelry, there is almost no chance that it will leave a green ring on your neck. But on the other hand, look-alike jewelry has made such great strides that the wise investor has a whole new set of pitfalls to beware.

One of these danger areas can be traced directly to this age of the designer and stylist. The popular demand for "new, creative, and exciting" designs has brought many new, creative, and exciting people into the jewelry business who know very little about the stones they use. Recently, for example, I looked at a topaz ring made by a new designer whose work is sold by the best stores and advertised in the best magazines. It may have been a creative and exciting ring. But it wasn't topaz, which is a precious stone that can cost as high as $100 per carat for a 10-carat stone. It was instead topaz quartz, a fairly common mineral with about the same hue and tone, which costs about $5 or $6 per carat, even for a good 10-carat stone. And I mentioned that fact out loud.

The designer's partner in charge of the display was incensed at the suggestion, and said angrily, "We use only the best stones." But on further, calmer discussion it turned out that she had never heard of the difference between the precious and the look-alike quartz topaz—and neither had four out of seven salespeople whom I queried later in jewelry departments of several large stores.

Look-alikes in the jewelry store are nothing new, of course. For years aquamarine and its cousin, the emerald, have been sold out of the same shop window. So have the unrelated red pair, ruby and garnet. For most people, there is no confusion at all among such gemstones. Everybody seems to know what those names mean, or at least that is the theory. In practice it's much, much wiser to ask. Don't count on your own knowledge or on the salesman's volunteering the information.

In addition to the familiar stones and look-alikes, many stores lately have begun to carry jewelry made of stone with names such as tanzanite, rhodocrosite, and tanjeloffite. To judge by the display space and promotion budgets, these stores do a handsome Christmas business with chunks of rock that look like petrified melon halves. But what are they, and how can you find out? Only by asking the salesman. But you must persist until the question is answered, as the following conversation recorded at a tanzanite counter illustrates:

"As you can see," the salesman explained, holding up a chunk of tanzanite, "it is very much like sapphire."

"So it's a sort of sapphire, then?"

"No," he said, "it's the same kind of stone as an emerald, except that it has a different color and is much cheaper."

"Then how can it be the same kind of stone as an emerald?"

"Well," he said, "it's about the same hardness as an emerald."

"Maybe it's the name that's confusing. Is there another name for tanzanite?"

"Oh yes," he said brightly, "it's sometimes called tanjeloffite . . . ."

In addition to ignorance, novelty, and some outright misrepresentation in the jewelry market, there is also the pitfall of investment-for-profit. That danger lurks behind every stone, but most especially in the diamond department.

"It may look like a diamond," in the words of a leading merchant in this market. "It may cut like a diamond. It may, in fact, be a diamond. But there's no guarantee that you'll ever make a profit if you resell it. There are all sorts of things involved in just getting your original investment back on most diamonds. You have to take into account the whole economy, the state of the diamond market, what kind you've got, and so forth.

"If you're buying a diamond for investment for profit," he said, "don't buy a stone under 10 carats. Ask Richard Burton. He knows."

For most diamonds of average size and quality, the market is carefully controlled by the mining interests such as DeBeers and others. And being a man-made market, diamonds are forever only as long as nobody rocks the boat.

Now, where does all of this leave a buyer shopping for jewelry? With only two safeguards, but big ones.

First, don't buy a gemstone of any size, description, or name unless you know exactly what it is—and have it all in writing from the store. Those written documents stand up wonderfully in court. And second, you have to know something about what makes quality, value, and negotiability in jewelry before you set foot into the marketplace.

Gold

As I said, you don't have to worry about your neck turning green. But there's still one adage that holds true: all that glitters is not gold. And, in fact, all that's gold isn't necessarily worth much. The range of prices of gold adornment is so wide that the mind reels. An 18-carat pin can cost $75, or it can cost $500, or it can cost anything in between. The metal itself, no matter how precious, is a secondary consideration in jewelry. Gold, platinum, or tin, the important thing is the design and execution. And that depends on how much handwork has gone into the finished piece, and—for some strange reason—how old it is.

Handmade objects are so costly nowadays, however, that almost no jewerly is made from scratch except for those few pieces with precious stones costing thousands of dollars. For the most part, handwork is kept to a minimum, and usually restricted to the finishing touches on a casting. The more of these finishing touches, the more expensive the final piece will be. Similarly, the older it is, the more likely it is to be expensive. But those two considerations have nothing to do with quality. Just because a piece is old, that does not make it good or well-made. And conversely, because it is new and has been cast from a mold, that does not make it poor quality. Ancient Egyptian jewelry, for example, was certainly handmade. But it looks as though it were turned out by a high school class in arts and crafts. Yet each time a piece turns up on the market, it is snapped up by a buyer in minutes. In either case, old or new, the gold itself is the last consideration. But it is a consideration, so the wise investor will have to be acquainted with the kinds of gold available in jewelry as well as with the usual methods of working it. To begin with the metal itself and new jewelry:

24-carat gold. Solid gold, and much too soft to use.

18-carat gold. 18 parts of gold to six parts of alloy, generally the standard of the finest gold jewelry. The alloy gives the gold rigidity and strength as well as hue. White gold is gold mixed with silver. In yellow gold, the alloy is brass. In pink, the gold is mixed with copper.

14-carat gold. That means 14 parts of gold to 10 parts of alloy. This is the minimum U.S. standard for gold jewelry. For some people, the higher alloy content produces an allergic reaction, discoloring the skin where it touches the metal. On the plus side, 14-carat gold, being stronger, can be lighter than its 18-carat counterpart.

Gold-filled. A base metal, usually brass or copper with no gold in it, forming a filling between a sandwich of gold. The outer layers are usually added by a mechanical process rather than by electroplating. By weight, one-tenth or one-twentieth of the piece is gold, and it is so marked—"1/10 G.F." or "1/20 G.F."

Gold-plated. A base metal—and sometimes plastic—to which a thin coating of gold is added by electroplating. The object is usually fashioned of the base substance first, and then it is plated with gold. On the other hand, gold-filled metal is constructed first and then the piece is fashioned from it.

Casting. Jewelry shaped in a mold, then soldered together and hand-finished. The finer the piece, the more separately molded pieces there are. Make sure the solder is as hard as the rest of the piece. Make sure there are no rough or uneven marks left by the mold. Look for evidence of hand-finishing on the back as well as on the front of the jewelry. You're paying for the workmanship.

Die stamping. The cheapest method of jewelry making.

The metal itself must be thin and light enough for a machine to punch it out and other machines to finish it.

Antique Jewelry

The following conversation comes verbatim from a recent antique jewelry show near Boston where money was changing hands faster than the eye could see. A woman buying a small golden pin for $75 inquired, "Now, you're sure this is a real antique?"

"Madam," the dealer reassured her, "you will have my written guarantee that it is genuine Pinchbeck."

If Christopher Pinchbeck had been alive to see that transaction, he would have turned over in his grave. Genuine Pinchbeck is his eighteenth-century alloy of copper and zinc designed to look like real gold. And that pin, when it was new, probably sold for a dollar or two.

When it comes to antique jewelry, people are willing to go out and buy with less knowledge than they buy either antiques or jewelry.

The reason is easy to discover at any show or sale.

For one thing, the craftsmanship bespeaks a time when things were painstakingly handmade. And for another, the passing years have put the stamp of enduring fashion on each item. A woman who wears an antique jet brooch doesn't have to worry about whether it is in good taste.

At least that is the theory.

Real life is another matter, as the following catalogue of the antique jewelry market will show.

Mourning jewelry. Always black, sometimes made of onyx, but more frequently of jet—a variety of hard coal. Worn by Victorian ladies to signify a death in the family. Neither fact seems to deter the growing market and rising prices in this grim adornment.

Old pearls. Compared with a diamond, the life of a pearl is brief—no more than 200 years before it deteriorates, loses its luster and color, and becomes only a sentimental investment for your heirs and assigns.

Seed pearls. These tiny pearls have the same life span as their larger relatives. But labor costs being what they are nowadays, there is no seed pearl jewelry made anymore. Scarcity may keep the value of this jewelry up regardless of deterioration.

Antique precious stones. For color and brilliance, most old diamonds, rubies, and emeralds are not in a class with their modern counterparts because the best methods of cutting precious stones were not perfected until the twentieth century. Both of these facts affect the resale value.

Memento mori. A latin phrase reminding us that in the end all must die. In old jewelry the term usually defines a brooch, necklace, or bracelet containing a lock of hair of the dear departed. That this kind of jewelry is considered in good taste is not surprising. The eighteenth century's ghastly fascination with the hair of the dead is just about the same as the twentieth century's fascination with the hair of the living.

Old gold. Can be exquisitely detailed and finely wrought. So can gold jewelry made yesterday. But the new doesn't have the romance and sentiment of having had another life, which seems to add to the value.

Cameos. The delicate carving of yesteryear is not available in today's cameos. The handwork has given way to mechanization. And it is too costly to look for the most beautifully veined agate or carnelian. Today's cameos are found mostly on shell and stones selected for adequacy rather than rarity.

Enameling. Another old art. And while modern enamels can be beautiful, the color seldom equals the old for naturalness and depth of tone. If you find an antique enamel that needs repair, don't count on getting a perfect match.

Miscellaneous junk. Cheap lockets by the thousands were made in the last century. So were artificially colored stones, such as turquoise dyed bluer or greener, depending on the fashion of the day. For years, Pforzheim, Germany, thrived by making copies of English jewelry in 4-carat gold. Much of that work has survived, and a lot of it is for sale in the antique market at enormous prices because under the law it is antique. But there is nothing in the law that says you have to buy it.

Under the circumstances, it is impossible to say for sure what any piece of antique jewelry should cost, or how the price compares with jewelry made yesterday.

Pearls

After years of being the adornment of female monarchs and graduating girls, the pearl is back in fashion. How it got back is no accident, because very little in the taste-and-fashion world is an accident. It has taken five years of hard work by the pearl industry to accomplish this victory. And so, with pearls having been made part of the fashion scene, the market has seen the arrival of "The Fashionable Pearl."

This fashionable pearl has everything that today's market in taste requires. It is big—but too big to be of very good quality. A perfect 10-millimeter cultured pearl of the finest luster and shape costs about the same as a 48-inch rope of similar size baroque fashionable pearls. It is also chic—but too chic to be timeless. "When styles change," says a leading distributor in the cultured pearl industry, "the fashionable pearls will have to be reset." And it is low priced—so low priced, in fact, that a rope of cultured fashionable pearls is on a par with a rope of the simulated variety styled up to high fashion. In short, everything about the fashionable pearl bespeaks one word: temporary. That is no news in the fashion world, of course. But it marks a noteworthy change in the world of pearls. Until quite recently, pearls were divided along three simple lines:

The natural pearl. Made by the oyster without any encouragement from anybody else. A rare and very expensive pearl. Natural pearls are one-of-a-kind, not necessarily completely round, and cannot be matched easily. Depending on size, these rare pearls can cost $100,000 or much more, depending on size, origin, and how things are in the shipping or motion picture business at the moment.

The simulated pearl. Made by dipping a glass bead in a solution of herring scales to build up eight or nine layers. A pearl of no great price. A necklace of simulated pearls retailing for $100 probably cost $3 or $4 to make.

The cultured pearl. A cooperative venture between men who run the industry and the oysters who make the pearls by covering an irritant with a natural substance called nacre. While there have always been inferior cultured pearls produced for the low-end market, the general aim of the industry has been to achieve the beauty, perfection, and quality of the natural pearl.

With the arrival of the fashionable pearl, however, that direction has been changed in about half of the industry. Today, it appears, the aim of the real is to imitate the imitation. Under the circumstances, it is a bit absurd to talk about investing wisely in fashionable pearls. But it can be done, at least in part. So, in defiance of the spirit of Christmas Present, here are a few items to keep in mind:

Luster is the one most important quality that determines the value of a natural or cultured pearl, fashionable or not. Luster is not just a glow that reflects the light (which is all that simulated pearls do) ; it is a glow from within, and should be apparent even away from direct light. It should also be of uniform good quality from every angle and side of the pearl. If a pearl seems to blink at you as you hold it, don't buy it. The appearance of blinking is a sign that the oyster hasn't had time to put a thick enough coating on the mother-of-pearl bead center. If it blinks, you're looking through the coating to the bead.

Color is another indication of quality. Of the light-hued pearls, creme rose is the highest priced, being a universally sought tone. Chalky white is generally the color of pearls that have been left in the oyster for one season (it takes about three seasons to make a creme rose hue). But the chalky white does enjoy some popularity, according to one leading importer, among many who used to wear simulated pearls and have graduated to the real thing. There are also smoky gray pearls, and pearls with a blue hue. They are not necessarily inferior to the creme rose, but their popularity is highest in Europe. These colors haven't caught on in the United States.

Shape and size make up the third consideration in pearl buying. Round, or apparently round, is the highest quality and generally isn't found in "fashionable" pearls, which are more likely to be baroque—uneven and asymmetrical. But a lustrous baroque pearl is worth more than a dull, lackluster, round one. There is also the mabe (pronounced *ma-bay*), a half-sphere pearl that was grown on the oyster shell. The mabe, too, is judged by its luster, thickness, and color. A 10-millimeter pair of mabe earrings may cost $50 for a reasonable quality. A 17-millimeter pair can cost about $200. The third variety of size is the seed pearl. Contrary to public opinion, this is not the seed from which the larger pearl is grown, but is a fully grown pearl the size of seed. The labor cost in making jewelry from seed pearls is prohibitive in the United States, so most are imported, often from Mexico.

Lack of blemishes—bumps, cracks, discolorations—add to the quality and value of a pearl.

The lengths of string are the final factor in determining

the price of pearls. There is the dog collar (13 inches long);
there is the choker (14 inches); the princess (18 inches); the
matinee (21 inches); the opera (up to 28); ropes (5 to 6
feet); and bibs, which are multiple strands.

Putting the length, quality, size, and color together, you
can get a very wide price range to select from. For example,
an opera length of 8-millimeter pearls (each the size of a
large, fresh pea) can cost $25, or $1,000, or $2,000. If it's a
$25 rope, it's probably made of the chalky white pearls that
were left in the water for one season instead of three, and so
do not have a 1-millimeter covering of nacre over the center,
but only one-thousandth of a millimeter of covering. The
$1,000 rope, however, will probably be made with three-
season pearls of creme rose or pale pink hue. If it's a $2,000
rope, then the chances are that the individuals are gem pearls
—handpicked for being flawless and evenly matched in size
and hue.

It is of crucial importance to remember that pearls are
not man-made. They are oyster-made of living material. So
don't let anybody tell you they are forever. Two lifetimes is
about the most you can expect before the pearl loses its luster
and dries out. But 150 years should be enough for even the
most prudent purchaser. Just keep in mind that organic
material cannot be treated the way inorganic stones can be
handled. Make sure that the pearls are strung on double-
twisted silk, not on nylon thread which picks up dust from
the air—particularly quartz dust—and becomes an abrasive
that will begin to saw at the pearls. In addition, not only
should pearls be wiped off after each wearing, but they
should also be professionally cleaned every year or two.

As for being able to see the difference between qualities
of pearls, it doesn't take long to educate your eye. Go to a
fine jewelry shop and ask to see the various pieces in the full
price range. The differences will make themselves apparent

quite quickly. Department store counters are too busy for that kind of shopping. You can't learn much from a harried sales person who merely hands you five different ropes and says, "Here, dear. Pick what you like."

Like pearls, all jewelry should be kept clean. And while the risks are highest in cleaning organic gems, it's also possible to make a costly botch of cleaning the others. That means you should know something more about your jewelry investment than its quality and price.

Cleaning

Contrary to the general rule, the rule for art and beauty frequently seems to be that cleanliness is next to worthlessness. In some objects, such as old bronze and pewter, the dark tarnish of time enhances price, if not loveliness. In brass and copper, on the other hand, only the bright and gleaming are considered handsome. But generally, it often pays not to be too industrious about cleaning jewelry, because you may damage it forever or scour away the signs of age that must grow back before worth can be restored.

Silver jewelry, for example, tarnishes in the air. But beware before you clean. Some of the tarnish is often part of the designer's plan and gives the piece some of its form— which will wash away with too thorough a cleaning. Moreover, a cleaning preparation that contains cyanide can crack or discolor inset stones.

Gold jewelry carries the same risks as silver.

Hard stones, such as diamonds, emeralds, sapphires, and rubies, collect grease from both the air and the wearer. They should be cleaned in a pot of hot water mixed with a little ammonia. But keep them in a sieve and off the bottom of the boiling pot, which can get hot enough to crack them.

Pearls were once living matter and are still quite

porous. They will discolor if treated with a harsh cleaning agent. So, use very mild soap and water that is only warm. Don't soak pearls, and dry them immediately.

Amber and coral, like pearls, were once living matter. Clean them with a soft cloth. If necessary, dampen the cloth, but only slightly.

Turquoise, lapis lazuli, and malachite are also porous. If washed, they will dry out and the color will change. A dry soft cloth is the only cleaner to use. If they are scratched, do not try to polish them yourself. They must have professional buffing.

Antique decorative glass bottles and vials can become stained. Beware of forcing a brush inside, as it may crack the glass or get stuck irretrievably inside. A mixture of warm water and ammonia shaken vigorously and left standing in the vessel should remove the stains. If it does not, then add a few pieces of BB shot to the mixture and shake. If that doesn't scour the stains away, try the BB shot dry, but don't shake too hard.

Ivory stains and discolors with age. But it is porous, too, and should never be immersed or even washed with water. However, it can be steam-cleaned. Put the piece of ivory in front of a boiling kettle spout. When the piece is steamy, dry it with a soft cloth. If the stain persists, then take it to a jewelry store for professional cleaning.

Silver plate, vermeil, and silver gilt should be cleaned with a slower-acting polish than the kind you use on sterling. All polish takes some surface metal away in the cleaning, but the slower the cleaner, the less it probably takes.

Thirty years ago, as many fatigued Americans can easily remember, life was a lot slower. Fast transportation usually meant a train. If a woman in her social ramblings wanted to know the time, she usually had to ask. And as for youngsters, if they wore a watch at all, it was usually a $1.50 Mickey Mouse.

Since those days, of course, the United States has learned in no uncertain terms that time is money. Today an old pocket watch of the sort railroad men used to buy for $35 is selling for $200 or more on the antique market. That old, but not antique, Mickey Mouse watch that cost $1.50 is worth upward of $100 in good condition on the Attic Recent market. Women's watches have long since moved out of the timepiece category and into the fashion salon. And as for the little timekeeping machine itself, well, people who look at their wristwatches today may not be interested in knowing the time at all. Instead, they may be checking on the date, the day of the week, the phase of the moon, the hour in twelve other principal cities, the altitude, the barometric pressure, the amount of fuel left in the tank, or the length of time they've been under water.

Naturally this changeover to fashion and complexity has taken its toll on the consumer. He is, the timepiece industry reports, nonplussed by it all. One company, for example, offers to send its experts to any store anywhere to teach sales personnel about watch works, maintenance, etc., so that they can answer customers' questions. But most stores have turned down this offer of an education program, replying that the customers almost never ask questions about these things.

What do they ask about instead? Trade names, it seems. In the words of an executive of a world-renowned jewelry store: "The customer seems to think you can buy a watch the way you buy a car—by the name of the maker and the shine on the door and hubcap. But unlike car-buying, when a fellow goes out to get a watch, he seldom asks the man who owns one." Now that the watch has become fashion and novelty, it is bought by how well-styled the case, face, and band are. So far, however, the industry has not succeeded in convincing women who spend $300 for only a few seasons' wear in a dress to buy a new watch when the present one is old-fashioned. "But we're trying to change that," an ad man said, "with new designs and bigger campaigns."

Whether or not it succeeds, there may still be a few people who are interested in a watch that keeps time, works well, and will last at least half a lifetime. For that saving remnant, here are a few things to keep in mind in the watch market:

The works. The average watch has about 70 parts, many of them in motion with and against each other. Most of these parts are either not visible to the consumer's eye, or their quality is not evident without high magnification. But there are a few indications that are visible in making a judgment. To wit:

The face. The poor quality watches usually have a face that has been stamped out of thin material. In better watches it is either a painted face or else the numbers have been cemented or screwed on.

The polish. The quality of a watch depends to a large extent on the fit of the parts with each other, their smoothness, and the snugness with which they sit in the case. So, shake the watch gently to feel whether it sloshes around in the case. Ask the salesman to take it out of the case and look at as much of the works as you can see, comparing it with the fineness of polish in a more expensive watch.

The jewels. To keep the metal parts from wearing away as they work against each other, the bearing points are jewels. The more expensive the watch, the more jewels—and the better quality of jewel, usually a synthetic ruby. A good watch should have no fewer than 17 jewels; a self-winding watch, 21.

The cheapest watches are made without any jewels at all. They have instead what is called a pin-lever movement; and without any protection at the moving points the metal machinery soon wears thin, to the irrevocable detriment of the timekeeping mechanism. A step up from the poorest quality are watches made with some jewels at friction points —but not in the crucial area called the escapement. Without protection there, the watch will start to be vastly inaccurate in about three or four months.

These pin-lever watches have recently been upgraded by the styling of the cases and design of face and band. Some, in fact, carry the names of designer celebrities—and with them, the aura of "fashion" and therefore of expendability.

If you've got to have a fashion watch, don't pay any more than $15 or $25 for it. And when it begins to go wrong, expect to have the entire works replaced. Many watch repair people will work only that way, because they can't guarantee a small repair on a pin-lever movement. Just remember that some jewels in the works are better than none.

The added attractions. Being capable of telling the day, date, phases of the moon, etc., does not necessarily mean that the watch has a fine movement.

Thickness. The thinner the case, generally, the more finely made the movement. But the thinner the parts, the more fragile they are.

The price. It's always dangerous to judge watch quality by the price tag. But don't look for bargains in the $20 to $40 price range. On the other hand, for above $75 you should expect a watch that doesn't vary by more than 30 seconds per day. And with a checkup every two years, it will last several decades at least. The danger in talking about price in this age of styling is that the real worksmanship may have gone into the case itself rather than into the moving parts.

In the intrinsic worth of a watch, the factors that count are invisible—the kind of metal used, the degree of polishing of parts, the precision work on the jewels, the quality of assembly of parts, and so on. To judge those factors, you simply have to rely on the jewelry merchant and on any consumer testing organizations in whom you have confidence. Consequently it's imperative to shop around, ask jewelers, friends, and watch repairmen for their opinions and judgments. Then, once you've decided on the watch you want, you can shop for differences in price. What you want may turn out to be for sale in a discount house—but not if it's a Swiss watch.

When the price of the watch depends to a great extent on the adornment—gems, precious metals, and the like—the first step is to establish the worth of the timepiece itself. Beyond that, you're out of the watch department and into the brooch and bracelet area, buying outright jewelry. The guides to buying that kind of watch are the same guides you use in buying any piece of jewelry.

Old Clocks

In the past several years there has been a ground swell of interest in old clocks. And that market is not only ticking more loudly each day, it is also chiming, bonging, chirping, and cuckooing. A nineteenth-century English mantelpiece clock that sold for $40 in 1958 is now priced at $175. An American oak kitchen clock made in 1910 has gone from $5 to $65 in the past five years.

Part of the reason, of course, is the very human interest

in the past and the Victorian-Edwardian era revival. But just as important a reason seems to be a changing national attitude toward modern, assembly line, split-second, infallible, precision living. Old clocks do not fit into today's scheme of home appliances. They require regular winding, occasional regulation, and—above all—personal care. And even then they are quite likely to be only sort of accurate. It's not a clock, one clock buyer after another reports, it's like having a living thing in the house.

So as you would expect, there is no evidence that buyers are having their old clocks electrified into perfect labor-saving devices, nor—in violation of the national pastime—are they being turned into lamps. Quite the contrary. As many dealers and repairmen report: "You ought to see the old junk people bring in to have put in working order. They don't care what the pedigree is. They don't care if the case needs refinishing. They don't care that grandma couldn't wait to get rid of that clock and get an electric model. All they want is a clock that goes tick-tock and more or less tells the time of day."

However, there are a few things that can make a clock buyer's quest somewhat easier, whether he's going to spend $35 for an old school clock or $750 for a grandfather clock.

➔Old French and English clocks frequently have a more finely made mechanism than the old American. But the old cuckoo clock, no matter where it was made, is usually a bad bargain, because it was made originally as a low quality clock.

There is no list price for old clocks. The tag is made out according to what the market will bear. So try to bargain.

➔Old clocks, like new ones, were made to run. Machine-made parts run better than stamped parts, which tend to get warped and bent in the stamping process.

➔Old clocks were not made to be moved. They should be set absolutely level—whether on floor, shelf, mantel, or wall—and kept there. A move means a readjustment.

➔Old clocks can go tick-tock, or tock-tock, or tick-tick. But if your's goes tick-*tock*, it's in need of attention.

IX

The Taste Business

O*NCE* upon a time it was a very easy matter to find out what was in good taste. All you had to do was to look at how the emperor lived, and then do the same if you could afford it. And you only had to do it once. Castle architecture seldom varied, and the imperial colors never. Here and there an emperor might be excessive in his demands for new clothing styles, but he was usually cured of that soon enough. By and by, however, emperors were no longer in good taste, and that day of taste leadership came to an end.

In the day that followed it, all you had to do to find out what was in good taste was to look at how polite society lived—the wives and daughters of shipping magnates, steel tycoons, and robber barons—and then do the same if you could afford it. Generally that was only once in a lifetime, too, or twice at the very most. If taste changed, it was on the rare occasions when the rich hired a new architect or upholsterer. But the day of that establishment has come to an end as well. Nowadays it's a breach of etiquette to mention good taste in polite society.

Well, who is in charge of taste today? According to cultrue reporter Alvin Toffler, "Taste used to filter down. Now it filters up from the young and middle class by way of the mass media. Look at the impact of a magazine like *Playboy* and the way of life it sells." But taste historian Russell Lynes disagrees. "Traditionally taste has been made by the magazines," he told me, "but most of them are gone. Today the magazines' impact on taste has been replaced by faster forms of communication such as window displays and manufacturers' advertisements." But is it the manufacturer who makes taste? "Manufacturers have neutral taste," said Milo Baughman, a leading furniture designer. "But the influence of those gaudy hotels at Las Vegas, Miami Beach, and Acapulco is tremendous. The rich see those places and take ideas home with them." So it's the rich who are in charge of taste? "No," said an editor at a famous decorating magazine, who naturally prefers to remain anonymous. "The rich are just as insecure as anyone else when it comes to taste. Ninety-nine percent of them have professional decorators . . ."

And so it goes, from observer to qualified observer, and adding up to what appears to be a perfect democracy with nobody in charge of taste at all. Looked at it in this way, you would think that the situation was only a matter of public opinion survey—a sort of average made up from everybody's ideals of beauty, with each man's taste as valid as the next.

But in actuality it doesn't work that way at all. As anyone in the fashion marketplace can tell you, the woman who may have no qualms about wearing a see-through blouse to the opera can be embarrassed into a frozen panic at the prospect of decorating her home. From the questions I have been asked at lectures and in mail from readers, it appears that the modern American girl may be very much emancipated and certain of her values, but her living room is often tentative at best and frequently stands unfinished. As it turns out, a see-through blouse is not nearly as revealing of a woman as the taste she will have to expose for judgment when she puts her home together.

But who makes that judgment today? Not the emperor. Not the society dowager. And certainly not public opinion, which has enough to do choosing political candidates and Academy Award winners without worrying about Hepplewhite, Eames, dusty pink, or forest green.

Sooner or later, however, anyone who invests in beautiful things will have to come to grips with this question of who is in charge of taste today. Not in order to find out and then follow. On the contrary, we have passed that day and good riddance to it. If you want beautiful things and you want them to stay beautiful, you have to choose them by your own standards and ideals of taste. But that is a very hard rule to follow unless you are sure that those standards and ideals are yours. So you should know who is in charge of taste today, and what their values are.

The plain fact is, there is a taste leadership. The vacuum left by those departed duchesses and dowagers has been filled by just what you'd expect in this day and age—experts and professionals. They go by such names as decorators, designers, stylists.

Item. Many of the better furniture houses are now making two kinds of their "best" wares. You can buy one in the store. You can buy the other only through an interior decorator.

Item. More and more fabric makers are putting effort

into new colors, designs, and construction that will be sold only through decorators' supply houses.

Item. In large cities an increasing number of home furnishings showrooms and shops are closed to consumers—unless they come in with a decorator.

Item. In most house-and-home magazines, nine out of ten rooms pictured were done by decorators, and many of the items shown can be bought only through a decorator.

Well, it takes only elementary arithmetic to add these items up. The decorators—or interior designers, as they prefer to be called—have taken over a good bit of the choice necessary to the exercise of personal taste. In fact, the decorator has become so important and powerful in taste leadership that almost everybody else in the market asks to be kept anonymous in discussing the situation.

In the words of a representative of a high-priced furniture line: "The decorators want to get their supplies on an exclusive basis. It's their bread and butter. If they can't get exclusivity from us, they will boycott our line." A spokesman for a major carpet manufacturing firm added: "We would be very foolish not to go along with the system. The decorator is one of the most important people to appeal to these days." And, said an executive in a "to the trade only" showroom of lamps and lighting fixtures, "People who don't want a decorator run into a real shopping problem because so much merchandise and so many places are closed to the private consumer."

Under the circumstances, it's not surprising to find that the membership of the American Institute of Interior Designers—the AID—has doubled in the past ten years. The National Society of Interior Designers, started a decade ago, now turns away about 50 percent of the decorators who apply for membership. Interior decoration exerts so great an influence on what is made and sold today that many states,

among them New York, California, and Texas, are considering legislation that will approve and license designers—a
move, according to many observers, that will both regulate
their activities and give legal sanction to their power. All in
all, it appears that the decorator has arrived to stay.

In theory, of course, it is a comfort to the consumer to
know that an expert is at the helm of taste, or at least on the
bridge. But in reality, it is not easy to find many in the
marketplace who like the situation.

In theory, for example, the decorator knows what colors,
designs, and fabrics harmonize. But in practice, a spokesman
for a custom fabric house said: "About 75 percent of the
decorators I see here are so awful that it is unbearable to
work with them. They're like the lost sheep and don't know
what they want or why."

In theory, the decorator knows what effects can be
achieved with lighting and where to get the fixtures required. But in practice, says a lighting expert with a list of
credits two yards long: "The decorators I've met don't know
anything about lighting. It's a whole gray area to them. And
they don't know where to go for information." And, added
the head of the lamp department of a major department
store: "I've had a running battle with these house-and-home
magazines and the decorator rooms they do. They want to
photograph light fixtures that look right in the picture, and
that's fine. We like to oblige. But you ought to see the fixtures they borrow from us for the pictures. One of these
editor-decorators has admitted to me on several occasions
that she knows she's borrowed the wrong lamp for the setting, but 'it's so pretty' that she can't help herself."

In theory, the decorator's expertise is worth his price. As
several clients have told me, "It's worth it to me to pay their
10 percent more to know that I'm getting a genuine antique
Hepplewhite chest." But in practice, said an antique dealer

and auctioneer who sells to the trade daily: "The decorators who come here have a real eye for color. And maybe they know style. But when it comes to furniture—forget it!"

Now, this is not to say the gap between theory and practice is always so wide in the world of the interior designer. Like any profession, this one has a broad spectrum of practitioners, ranging from very good to very bad. But like any profession, their expertise is unquestioned. As one antiques dealer put it: "A customer may argue with me about my price of $600 for a carved wood mantel. But if a decorator buys it and then sells it to him for $1,900, he never dreams of complaining."

Like any profession, too, interior design has developed its own branches and specializations. One such is the kitchen designer who, for a fee, tells you what kinds, colors, and styles of appliances and cabinets your kitchen should have, and then sees to it that they are installed in the proper places. For those who think that may not be a good way to earn a living, it should be pointed out that 20 years ago there were about 300 kitchen designers in the United States. Today there are over 12,000. And, moreover, at least one university is offering a two-year course in kitchen design now.

How this specialty of interior decoration has prospered is easily explained, and illustrates how the entire profession has moved into a position of taste leadership.

Part of the reason, of course, has been the affluence of the past several decades. In the words of a secretary who was waiting to talk with her kitchen designer about putting a $6,000 kitchen in her $26,000 house: "Well, there's no use putting the money into a third car. The children are still too young to drive."

Another reason for the rise of this specialty of interior decoration is the new status that attaches to the kitchen. In the words of a suburban housewife with a new $10,000 designer kitchen: "You don't buy a Rolls Royce only because it's a long-lasting car. Utility is just one small part of it."

In addition to considerations of affluence and status, a very tangible problem confronts people who are furnishing and decorating. Finding your way through the maze of cubic footage, gallons per second, ice cubes per minute, and meteorite-resistant finishes is as overwhelming to many as unraveling the mysteries of sterling silver, Oriental rugs, and bone china. In the words of a schoolteacher looking through a kitchen design showroom: "It's as hard as deciding which new car to buy."

The last, and perhaps most important, factor in the rise of professionally designed kitchens is the current tempo in fashion that changes seemingly from minute to minute, until the dancers can no longer tell if they're in step. In the words of an executive of a titanic appliance manufacturing corporation: "At least 10 percent of the nation's population remodels its kitchen every three years. After all, you wouldn't drive your car for longer than that."

Like the rest of the decorating profession, kitchen designers can appeal to every pocketbook. A spokesman for the kitchen designers' professional association, for example, explained in detail the wide price range available from "a VW kitchen to a Cadillac kitchen."

And so, not surprisingly at all, designer kitchens are sold just about the same way cars are sold. In the words of one independent designer: "Customer choice has very little to do with function or utility or performance. It's the drawings I do that sell them—the Before and After, in color, of course. They can't resist it if it's art."

Now, none of this is the final word on the subject. In both theory and practice many professional decorators in all specialties perform a worthwhile service. As one well-publicized decorator put it: "There are a lot of ignorant women with money to spend. They could be a lot less ignorant if they would read about style and design. But for some reason, they find that unthinkable."

For them, the professional seal of approval is very important. And they don't mind living with somebody else's style and taste in order to get that approval. But that's not the only reason for the importance of the professional decorator, stylist, and designer.

As everybody knows, it is not really in good taste to talk about the t - - - - t in public.

In 1965, however, Professor Alexander Kira of Cornell University threw caution to the winds and published his detailed study of the subject. It was a frank report simply entitled, "The Bathroom." And in it, Professor Kira pointed out the obsolescence, discomfort, unsanitariness, and outright danger frequently found in this room and its unmentionable fixtures. Among the items revealed in this study were:

The sink too low for most people over the age of 12; the water-closet seat too high for natural functions and too small for grown-ups; the bathtub seemingly made for use by people without vertebrae, and for cleaning by contortionists; showers with taps placed so that you have to reach through cascades of water to adjust temperature and flow; laundry hampers that keep dirty clothes constantly damp; slippery tub bottoms; the use of a bidet mentioned only by the very thoughtful or the very naughty; and the room itself a standard, cramped 5 by 7 feet. No other room, the Kira study suggested, has been so neglected. People who would not put up with a carpet beater or washboard today are using just

about the same kind of bathroom engineering they had 70
years ago.

Well, in the years since the Kira study came out, the
U.S. bathroom industry has responded to the findings in a
remarkable way.

"Suddenly bathrooms are living rooms!" sings the head-
line of a recent product brochure from a major fixture manufacturer. The booklet goes on to explain how you, too, can
have sensuality, escape, and the choice of 132 decorator
colors in your bathroom.

"The big news in bathrooms now," a showroom salesman said proudly, "is bone color. If you want to be sure of
good taste, decorate your bathroom in bone. Those in the
know will recognize that you paid top dollar."

"We're featuring a completely new bathroom," said a
spokesman for the most luxurious bath shop in the country.
"It's totally faced in marble. Of course the basic engineering
isn't new in any important way. But then, this is one room
people don't really want to change."

Sinks are still too low and seats still too high and small.
But now there are lovely crystal chandeliers, wall-to-wall
carpeting, and faucets, shower heads, and water handles in
Early American and Eagle motifs. For the most part, tubs are
still made for the infinitely plastic, and you still have to
reach through the falling shower water to adjust the temperature and flow. But on the other hand, you can now decorate
your bathroom to look like almost anything from a Mediterranean villa breakfast room to a London townhouse library.
According to an executive with the National Association of
Bath Manufacturers, Americans are now spending ten times
more money on the bathroom and its decor than they did
before the Kira study was published.

Professor Kira did not appear to be surprised at the
industry's response to his suggestion that re-engineering was

needed. "In the first place," he told me, "you can't revolutionize a billion-dollar industry overnight. Especially not when it is set up to work in cast iron, a material that can't be worked in sheets large enough to make immediate changes. That change requires working in plastics. But it takes a long time to retool. And with the cost of home building going up all the time, contractors want to keep expenses low. So naturally they would rather continue with the old standards as long as possible."

But in the second place—and just as important, Professor Kira pointed out—is the national reluctance to discuss the bathroom and its appliances openly. Executives in the industry are worried, and reasonably so, about the advisability of changing the selling concept and starting to talk about physiological needs and safety to the consumer in addition to the usual sales message about styling and design.

Under the circumstances, the plumbing industry has naturally balked at introducing a change. It has been much less expensive to leave undisturbed the public sense of propriety regarding the t - - - - t, and a lot more profitable to offer 132 decorator colors and a French style chandelier instead of a nonslip tub, a bidet, and a lower-seated, odorless euphemism.

When it comes to priorities, even in this technological civilization, the scientist and engineer aren't always the leaders. The stylist, designer, and decorator are frequently in the driver's seat. And for very good and money-making reasons. Unless you're aware of their position and influence, it's sometimes difficult to be sure that you're listening to your own convictions, ideals, and standards of taste.

※

Public opinion may not be able to make taste. But what it can make, and make very well, is a celebrity. And so the landscape of style, design, and decoration abounds with celebrities today. In clothing design, for example, it is hardly a novelty to see a girl on the street wearing a dress signed visibly by Pucci, a head scarf autographed "St. Laurent," shoes bearing the ornament "C.D." for Christian Dior, and a coat displaying a "V" for Valentino. There are likewise celebrities in hair styling, chair design, room decoration, and so on.

Generally speaking, the taste celebrity can be distinguished by two characteristics, both of them very appealing at the polls.

In the first place, the taste celebrity is almost never known as an artist or even as a craftsman, because both of those terms require everybody's agreement about standards and accomplishments. So he is usually known as a stylist, designer, decorator, or other flexible professional title implying that he is not only capable but also ready and willing to restyle, redesign, and redecorate when public taste has changed. And consequently, his achievements are not known as either art or craft, but rather as "new," "different," "exciting," and/or "creative."

The second requirement of the taste celebrity is, of course, that he be a celebrity. And that means being celebrated everywhere in taste leadership. Until quite recently, for example, a clothing designer's name on perfume bottles was his bread and butter. (His name on clothing was his swimming pool.) And, in fact, a Wall Street and Paris investment banker said candidly: "We were planning to buy the house of Courreges at one time. But we decided against it finally because he didn't have a line of perfume with his name. All he had was his name. It was a bad mistake on our part to abandon the proposition. If we had only seen the trend, we could have bought him and put his name on a line of dining room furniture one of our companies manufactures."

In this day of the taste celebrity, the rule seems to be that if it was designed by a designer, whatever it is, then it must be worthwhile. And if it doesn't appear to be worthwhile, then the ailment is in the beholder and consumer. Just how worthwhile a designer's work is can be seen most clearly in the clothing industry, where a moderately well-known designer earns a salary of about $50,000 plus a royalty of between 15 and 25 percent on the sale of his line of clothes, plus the extras from work for plays, movies, linen manufacturers, drapery houses. As large, if not larger, than these sources of income is the franchise business which puts his name on other products to help them sell.

One very successful designer is frankly worried about this rising influence of the taste celebrity. He is Jack Lenor Larsen, whose influence in textile design is seen in homes, offices, and airplanes, and whose clients have included such executives as the President of the United States. What worries Larsen is the possible consequence of power without responsibility that often comes to such celebrities.

"If all those designers actually designed all of the different things their names appear on," he said to me, "they wouldn't have time to eat or sleep." Mentioning the name of a world-renowned clothing designer, Larsen said, "I wonder if he's seen the line of towels yet that he's supposed to have created."

This cavalier attitude toward both the product and the consumer reverberates throughout all of design, and can be detected clearly among young designers starting out in the field, Larsen said. "Many of these young people couldn't care less. If they want to do a stockbroker's office in orange and purple, it's awfully hard to stop them. One gets the feeling that they've forgotten about everybody else and that they're designing for themselves alone."

That accent-on-youth combined with taste-by-celebrity

can also be seen in the current state of the crafts. "Young designers don't begin to reach the height of their creativity until they're past 30," said Larsen, winner of the Craftsmanship Award of the American Institute of Architects. "Before 30, their work tends to be very derivative. They think that if they're copying creative work, they are being creative, too." But in the new, creative, exciting world of design—and in the world that surrounds it in search of taste leadership—there's nobody to tell them what the score really is. Creativity and excitement are very flexible criteria, and really useful only to whip up the opinion of the people who make public opinion take notice.

But if the taste celebrity can exercise his power without responsibility, Larsen said, it couldn't have happened without help from the consumer. "Most women dress better than they furnish their homes. When it comes to dressing the house, they are awfully timid—with one exception. And that is in buying sheets. Then nothing can be too far out. Why? Because no mother-in-law will ever see the bed linen."

Whether it is a mother-in-law or some indefinite "they" who sit in judgment is beside the point. The real question is: where do "they" get their standards of taste? Who sets their ideals for them? As I said some pages back, anybody who wants to invest in beautiful things and have them remain beautiful will sooner or later have to come to grips with this question. For the wise investor, the answer is a personal and individual one. But you can't arrive at it without having taken a good look at the taste-making machine and how it works.

What type of music do you find most enjoyable?
What type of carpeting do you find the most pleasing?

How to Invest in Beautiful Things

Which movie star do you most enjoy seeing perform?
What kind of draperies do you prefer?
What kind of magazine do you read regularly?

Those, of course, are questions of individual taste. Asked by the proper expert in the proper way, order, and quantity, they should add up to an individual's taste. At least that is the theory in this scientific age of reducing everything to its smallest particular, counting it, measuring it, and feeding the result into a computer to get the answer. Approached that way, the taste machine should be able to tell you not only what colors and furniture will please your eyes, but also which spouse to marry in order to keep the motif harmonious. All in all, it is the logical consequence of professional taste leadership in this technological civilization, and could make a very nice motion picture starring Peter Sellers, Groucho Marx, Mae West, and Univac. But as it turns out, it's too late for that.

There is already a computerized industry for matching men and women with the object of matrimony. And now, in a pilot project that Burlington Industries says is getting wonderful results, those questions listed above and 21 others like them are being put to customers in department stores, the answers fed into a computer, and lo! the machine replies with a complete plan for furnishing and decorating the house.

Burlington House president Ray Kassar sees all kinds of prospects for this computerized taste counseling service, as well as the answers to most of the perplexities facing the consumer nowadays. "Women are terribly frustrated about furnishing their homes," he said. "And so they end up fighting with their husbands. The computer, however, takes away all those problems. The machine becomes the arbitrator." Furthermore, it is a great boon to the store itself. "After all, sales help is very hard to get. And frequently sales people don't know, or don't want to know, what they're selling."

There are two additional advantages to this method that put it squarely in the mainstream of taste-making today. First, the decorating plans in the computer's repertoire will eventually be commissioned from the nation's best-known stylists and designers. "If the idea catches on," Kassar said, "in a couple of years mass market women will be able to have their interiors designed by celebrities. Of course it won't be personal or individual counseling. But it will save a lot of women the embarrassment of having to show a decorator how they live." The second advantage of the plan is for the store that carries this computerized taste service. The answers that the electronic brain gives will draw only on what the store has in stock and is trying to sell. No matter how intelligent, the brain will not suggest any furnishings that can be bought only at some other store.

If there are any disadvantages in computerized taste, they are difficult to find. What if you change your preferences in movie stars or magazines? That doesn't matter in the least because the machine hasn't paid any attention to those questions and answers in the first place. What the circuitry actually works with are your preferences regarding formal or informal, warm colors or cool, antique or modern, etc. Those other items about actors and reading matter are only there to give the consumer a warm, moist glow of personal attention. What if a woman doesn't agree with the furnishing plan given by the computer? "She can take her questionnaire back," Kassar said, "change her answers, and requery the machine. If she still disagrees with the reply, she simply doesn't have to follow its instructions." And what if people object to the whole idea of computerized taste?

"In that case," Kassar said, "we may have to change the

name of the service, or leave the word 'computer' out of the title."

Whether or not the Burlington Industries computer taste service works, the basic situation remains unchanged. Professional and expert taste leads much of the market, and puts a lot of pressure to conform on individual standards and ideals. In the words of a woman well past 80 who stopped to chat with me after a lecture recently: "There's certainly a lot more in the stores than there was when I was a bride. But it seems to be more of the same things. There really isn't any more choice of the different things or different styles. And I have the feeling that there's less choice than there used to be."

Well, yes and no. It is the wide choice that allows for the expression of individual taste. And a brief look in the marketplace seems to reveal a sad sameness to everything. But investing wisely in beautiful things requires more than a brief look in the marketplace.

True enough, in the textile industry computers are designing fabric and operating looms. In furniture factories 60 percent of production is in plastic, meaning that a machine can make a chair in less than a minute as long as it keeps making the same chair over and over again. In ceramics, mass production long ago overtook the potter's wheel—maintaining price and uniform quality at the expense of variety in design. In many industries electronic brains and nerves have made market surveying a matter of moments and have resulted in scientifically regulated production schedules and a narrower choice of styles in order to supply the greatest number at the lowest cost.

On the other hand:

➤A computer programmer in the textile industry who spends all of her spare time at work on a hand loom in her home has yet to use one of her carpets in her own home. "As fast as I can make them, they're sold and gone," she told me.

➤A dentist, who worked for two years in silver in order to learn enough to make a set of flatware for his wife's anniversary present, told me, "It turned out quite nicely. And I've had an offer to make more of it for a local jewelry store."

➤A retired physical education teacher who has learned the art of cabinetmaking since leaving the school system said: "I'm in my art nouveau period now. I'm surprised nobody is doing this kind of work in the big companies. It's not for every taste, I suppose. But I don't have any trouble selling it at all."

It's impossible to say exactly how widespread this revival in handcrafts is. But a spot check of six big cities reveals that each has more than a dozen craftsmen's groups and associations. Of a dozen universities queried, five are now giving both undergraduate and graduate degrees in crafts, and four are planning to do so in response to student interest. And makers of looms, kilns, and sophisticated wood-finishing materials report an overwhelming rise in sales and reorders. One of the nation's largest importers of pearls in California says that his offices are flooded with mail requesting information on jewelry making. "Don't ask me what's going on out there," he said. "But we're putting together a $10 kit and book on this subject. And there's nothing for the amateur about it." And, added a researcher at the American Craftsmen's Council, "This movement has grown so fast in the past seven or eight years that there is no way to keep track of it. In fact, it's hard to keep up with the day-to-day increase in our own membership. And we admit only people with professional status."

The reasons for this burgeoning handcrafts industry vary from craftsman to craftsman, naturally. A men's clothing store owner whose spare-time metalwork sells as fast as he can make it said: "It's not for money. What I make would never support me. But there is a route to sanity in it." Said the president of one craftsmen's group: "I used to be a potter. But I finally decided that the mass producers could do it better than I. So I switched to weaving. You can do things on a hand loom that the automated machines can't. And that's real satisfaction to me." And, said a retired salesman who is now a very busy bookbinder, "I suppose it has something to do with having a creative activity. But I don't really know. When you are very busy, you don't have time to wonder about the philosophical reasons."

But the best, and perhaps summary reason, for this renaissance in crafts was stated by a woman at a crowded show where she had just bought a cashmere scarf from a full-time insurance salesman who keeps his part-time loom in his bedroom. "You see," the woman said, beaming with pleasure at her new scarf, "it's handmade. Not homemade. Not machinemade. But actually handmade."

But finding these craftsmen and their shows is not as easy as driving out to the shopping mall. It requires not only inquiry, but persistent inquiry. Since 1957, for example, the sterling silver industry has conducted an annual Sterling Silver Design Competition. But nobody has ever heard of the winners—and very likely nobody ever will. After the annual awards they simply disappear back into the oblivion of their craft, or take their awards with them into the anonymity of a job with a major sterling factory. The plight of the silver designer-craftsman is the plight of the independent designer-craftsman in furniture, glass, porcelain, and the other arts and crafts of the civilization. And what stands between them and an investor in beautiful things is often the civilization itself.

"It took me a year to make a set of flatware," said a

silversmith from New York State. "Maybe people would wait a year for their flatware in Paul Revere's time. But they won't wait these days. It's hard enough for them to pick a pattern they think is in good taste without having to worry about their decision for a year before it's delivered."

Said a silver designer from Virginia: "I really wouldn't begin to know what to charge for this bowl. I know what it would cost if it were made by a factory—that is, if they wanted to go to all that trouble. But I couldn't charge that much. After all, I'm not a factory. I'm just a person."

Said an Ohioan who won a recent Design Competition with a set of sterling goblets: "How would I describe the stems? Well, I don't know. I made them so they couldn't be described. I made them so they had to be seen and felt to be understood."

But if the independent craftsman-designer has trouble reaching the public, he has even more trouble reaching the stores. A spokesman for Tiffany & Co., in the usual tradition of lamenting the end of a bygone era, said: "I wish we could do something to encourage the rebirth of American silversmithing. But it is hopeless. American silversmithing is too artsy-craftsy. So we have to employ silversmiths from Poland, Turkey, Italy, and Spain." What about the Design Competition, or the work in sterling being done at Alfred University, Cranbrook Academy, the Cleveland Art Institute —well, the man from Tiffany & Co. had never seen any of that, he explained.

A spokesman for Cartier's said: "We want to encourage silversmithing, of course. But almost no one is doing any in America." Did he know that the Museum of Contemporary Crafts at 29 West 53rd Street in New York, a half-block away from his store, had a file of several hundred Americans presently working in silver? No, he said, he did not know that.

And so, the independent designer-craftsman in silver,

like his counterpart in other fields of beauty, is condemned
to wait until the consumer looks for him. Creativity and
talent and craftsmanship, it appears, are not enough without
celebrity status in addition.

Or, to put it another way, an expression of individual
taste requires some expenditure of individual energy and
time. It's fruitless to wait for beautiful things to come to you.
That sort of practice went out with the dowager and duchess.
A choice of style, design, art, and craftsmanship are still with
us. But you have to look for them.

To put it still another way, if Paul Revere were alive
today, he would almost certainly be working in silver. But
his name would also be on cars, chairs, shoes, jewelry, air-
plane interiors, kitchens, and a complete line of "1776 Fashions" for Nieman-Marcus and other leading stores coast to
coast.

X

Table and Room Settings and Lighting

*F*ROM the intimate wine to the intricate dessert, it was everything the traditional romantic dinner should have been. And naturally it was served by candlelight. When it comes to beautiful things, the setting is as important an investment as the objects they surround. The color and the lighting may not be expensive items in the budget—a small number of candles cost only a few pennies after all—but knowing how and where and when to use them can make an investment in beauty speak its true worth.

Well, to continue, it was a romantic dinner and naturally it was served by candlelight. And so, naturally, she was getting a splitting headache, and he was getting a terrible case of heartburn. And as for her brilliant *moussaka* served on old Imari, and his imported *Hermitage* in Baccarat crystal, they were lost in the flickering shadows. Fashions in menu, charm, and salad oil may come and go. But for some reason beyond human understanding, the rite of the candle-lit dinner seems to endure forever.

Why this myth persists in the present incandescent age is anybody's guess. A number of psychologists suspect that it is like the continuing allure of the roaring wood fire in an open fireplace, and probably has its roots deep in man's primitive reliance on flame. But whether that is really so is open to question. After all, you never hear even the most romantic or primitive say, "Darling, isn't the falling snow beautiful? Let's turn off the furnace and build a fire in the fireplace." But somehow when it comes to dinner, nobody thinks twice about turning off all the lights and illuminating the table with only a pair of candles—set in eighteenth-century English Matthew Boulton candlesticks, of course.

In this particular setting, the theory seems to be that candlelight is not only good for the hostess's complexion and a stimulant for marvelous table conversation, but along with good cooking it is also the surest way to a man's heart. In real life, however, it doesn't work out that way at all. In a darkened room, as any hypnotist can tell you, a single small light acts as a distracting barrier to vision, rather than as an illumination. For people who wear eyeglasses, and especially those who wear contact lenses, the reflection of a dancing candle flame can be downright uncomfortable. And whatever candlelight may do for a lady's complexion, it can undo with the Lady Macbeth shadows it throws around her eyes. According to a continuing casual survey made by lighting expert Elizabeth Meehan, "Men simply don't like to eat when they can't see the food." (It was a man, King Louis XV of France, who got the candles off the dinner table by inventing the chandelier.)

But despite all of that, the myth of the candle-lit dinner persists, as do quite a few others when it comes to setting and background, most especially when it comes to lighting. And as any witch doctor or interior decorator can testify, the trade in persistent myths is frequently very profitable.

If you want to open an expensive steak house and sell a lot of cocktails, you merely build a cave—black upholstery, somber paneling, dark carpets and, of course, candles on the tables, preferably in small red glass chimneys. There is something about a little island of dim light in the encroaching gloom that calls for another fortifying refill. If you can't get a liquor license, however, and have to make your restaurant pay off in a quick turnover of fast meals to fast eaters, you simply tile the establishment in white porcelain and flood the room with bright neon light. And if you want the gourmet trade, you make the lighting adequate and unobtrusive, and concentrate on finding a good chef.

But if all you want is an intimate, elegant dinner party, amidst a beautifully furnished room and table, then for heaven's sake:

➤Use at least six candles on the table for a party of four. Add another candle for each additional person.

➤Place your candles in two groups, one at each end of the table, not in the middle.

➤Use candlesticks or candelabra tall enough to put the candle flame well above eye level.

➤Light the corners of the dining room in order to dispel the suspicion of encroaching gloom. So, put another candelabrum on the sideboard or, if you can bring yourself to it, turn on a low wattage wall lamp. An easily installed wall switch with a rheostat built in will allow you to adjust the brightness of the bulb.

The traditional candle-lit dinner, with its flickering shadows and uncomfortable, distracting flame, is the perfect light to illuminate the problems of lighting the entire household setting. For all the development in bulb shapes and fixture styles, the American residence is still a dark cave filled with too many lamps and not enough light, or an overbright, harshly visible affair that forces the eyes to look at the floor for rest. In the words of Abe Feder, who has designed the lighting for Broadway shows, museums, concert halls, and the like:

"American women spend about $800 million each year on lamps, and another $500 million each year on makeup, and they can't see well enough to apply it properly. The fact is, 1,240 watts can light a room nicely, while 250 watts can be glarey and painful."

The fault, the home lighting industry admits, lies largely with itself.

"We lighting engineers," said a lighting engineer with Sylvania, "have been so concerned with separating tasks and lighting for them—reading, sewing, etc.—that we have forgotten to look at the room as a whole."

Said a spokesman for Duro-Lite, which makes a flickering flame-shaped bulb that gives the illusion of a burning wick: "I can't understand anybody's wanting to use this bulb. I don't see any real need or reason for it."

Said an executive at Leviton, a leading manufacturer of bulb sockets: "There are no independent underwriting laboratories testing this kind of lighting and electrical equipment. There are no standard specifications and requirements. Consequently, you can be paying $150 for a lamp and getting a socket that will burn out the proper bulb and force you to use one of a lower, inadequate illumination."

Said a spokesman at General Electric: "There's nothing new in home lighting largely because the industry can't get together. If a bulb manufacturer calls a seminar to discuss problems and solutions, many lamp-base makers won't attend unless the topic is specifically study lamps, say, or work lamps."

But if the makers of components have trouble getting together, so do the lamp designers, salesmen, and decorators who determine what will be available. Said a commercial photographer whose pictures of rooms and settings show up in many of the major house-and-home magazines: "When I come in for a job, I bring a thousand dollars worth of lights with me. The room is illuminated for the photo. In real life it doesn't look the same at all. You simply can't judge the effects of lamps when you see them in a picture."

Said a salesman in the showroom of one of the nation's largest lamp and lighting fixtures distributors: "Now, take this item—a gold base with a black shade. It's become very popular over the past few years since the decorators decided that it would give an accent to a room. But just try to tell customers that it won't give much light, and they get sore at you. A showroom is no place to find out what kind of illumination a lamp will give."

And, added a lamp designer who asked that he not be identified: "Our whole problem in lighting is that we think small. Table lamps. Cove lighting. Spotlights in the ceiling. Why, I've even designed a light to illuminate nothing but the draperies. We don't design lighting. We design decoration. And what do you end up with? Mushroom globes that glare in your eyes. Down lights that throw horrible shadows under your eyes, nose, and chin. And illuminated draperies— illuminated draperies? Why?"

And, added a home building contractor: "I guess you could say we think small, too. Families I've built homes for will spend $100,000 for the house and settle for $100 worth of lighting fixtures when they look over the plans."

Under the circumstances, creating the proper setting for beautiful things is not the easiest job in today's light-and-lamp market. You can't expect to find a selection of ready-made solutions to the problem in the fixture stores and departments. You just have to figure out what kind of setting you want and need, and then hunt for the proper hardware to do the job. To do so, however, there are several factors to keep in mind.

Lamp vs. Light

There is a vast difference between looking at a lamp and seeing by the light it throws. Never have those two differences been so confused as they are in today's market, where there is heavy emphasis on the source of light and very little on the kind of illumination it gives. As a result, it is easy to end up with a dim room punctuated by small or large pools of glaring light. Or, without careful planning, you can find yourself in a room that is bright enough to see in, but not to read, eat, sew, or talk in.

The primary objective in most home settings is an overall illumination with additional accents of lighting for different areas and tasks. The contrast should not be between dark and light, but rather between light and more light. (That seems obvious. But take a look at the homes of your friends to find out how it actually works.) To get an overall illumination, you will have to light the walls and, if possible, the ceiling. So, avoid opaque lamp shades as a general rule, and take a look at lamp attachments that will wash the ceiling and walls.

Highlighting

There are a number of fixtures that are used for pointing up an area or creating a special pool of light. Used carefully, they can make your investment in furnishings worth a hundred times the cost. But overdone or poorly done, these special effects lights are disastrous.

For example, ceiling spotlights are wonderful for illuminating paintings, the piano area, the dining table, etc. But if these spotlights hit the diners or the pianist, they will turn your family and guests into ghoulish caricatures, with shadows under eyes, nose, and chin. So, if the entire room is adequately illuminated, the spotlights need be only of low wattage and must be carefully aimed to hit only the table or keyboard-and-music. In spotlighting paintings, a different problem arises. If you follow the common tendency to over-light the pictures, the room begins to look like an art gallery with each work for sale. If you underlight the pictures, they become indistinguishable dark rectangles on the wall. The solution to the problem is a switch with a rheostat, allowing you to adjust the amount of light hitting the canvas.

For some reason, there is also a frequent urge to high-light the draperies. Why that is so is very hard to understand; some lighting experts think it comes from too much exposure to store and theatrical lighting. In any event, there are disadvantages to illuminating the draperies with special lighting. For one thing, it calls attention to a large, uninter-rupted area of wall for no particular reason. And for another, this kind of lighting usually requires a cool light—such as fluorescent, which often distorts the fabric color and re-sults in a completely upside-down illusion. There are really only two good reasons to highlight a wall of draperies apart from the overall room illumination. First, if they are a hand-painted fabric by Picasso, say, or some other amazing fabric, they should get specially dramatic attention. Or, second, if they are going to part and reveal Lily Pons about to sing.

Translated into language, highlighting or spotlighting says one word: "Look!" How loudly or sharply you want to say that depends on a number of things, among them your self-confidence.

Bare Bulb

As everybody knows, the incandescent electric light bulb that Thomas Edison invented was not a beautiful thing, what with its hot filament glaring out into the darkness. And so all sorts of shades and covers were invented to hide the bulb and diffuse its light.

Well, here it is almost a century later. And guess what: the lamp shade is now obsolete and the bare-bulb look is in. Whatever that says about the state of taste today, it also says a great deal about what designers think of consumers. The bare-bulb look is available at every price from $19.95 to $350. For $150 there is a lamp that looks like a stovepipe with the bare bulb pointing out at you like a finger. For $250 you can get a simple standing lamp topped off with a bare bulb. In between are low mushroom-shaped bare bulbs for the floor, and small tree-shaped bare bulbs for desk and table top. An executive in a large lamp store that carries a full range of these fixtures told me: "Of course I wouldn't have the bare-bulb look in my home. But this is what people want. And we're in business to give them what they want."

There is only one thing wrong with the bare-bulb look. It is apt to be treated as an object of art instead of as a light source, fitted with a fairly high-wattage lamp, and set in a fairly dim room. And as a result, it will behave as those candles on the table did—fixing the viewer's eye, distracting attention, and obliterating the remainder of the room and its objects. Once again it is a case of too much contrast between dark and light. In the words of a lighting fixture wholesaler: "If the people who buy these bare-bulb lamps find themselves uncomfortable, they'll probably never realize the reason for it. They'll decide that their walls are the wrong color, or that the draperies are the wrong texture. They'll change a lot of things in the room before they'll think of changing the lamp."

Chandeliers

For several centuries now the crystal chandelier has been the mark of elegance and luxury in the dining room. And despite all sorts of technological changes in lighting, the chandelier seems to hold on to its status. The reason, according to song, story, and advertisement, is that the reflection of light through the prisms and pendants of crystal makes the silver on the table glow and the food taste better. But whether that is so depends on a few basic items in the selection, installation, and illumination of the chandelier.

Whether it's *crystal* or *glass* makes a big difference in both the aura and the illumination. It also makes a big difference in the price. In the American market the word "crystal" can include glass. If you're paying crystal prices, make sure you're getting crystal with at least 24 percent lead oxide content. Crystal chandeliers begin at about $500, glass at about $75. There's nothing disreputable about a glass chandelier, just as long as you don't expect to get the same tone and glow that comes from crystal. And because glass doesn't have the depth of brilliance, its pendants have to be washed frequently. When cut glass gets dirty, it looks like a dirty window.

(In addition to glass and crystal there is also rock crystal. But unless you have $1,500 to spend on a small chandelier, forget this material. Unlike crystal, which is a manufactured high quality glass with a lead oxide content, rock crystal is a natural rock that has been mined. For all its status and price, however, rock crystal in chandelier pendants does not have the depth of color of lead crystal. In fact, dealers are having some trouble these days selling clear rock crystal chandeliers because they look too much like glass. On the other hand, the flawed, fissured, less desirable rock crystal is salable because there is no doubt about what it is. That is conspicuous status at its best.)

The pendants themselves should be judged by how they are cut—the more facets, the more varied the refraction of light. The full-cut pendant—with the same faceting on front and back—yields the best color. In addition, you should also look for hand-cut pendants, as they are capable of more intricate facets than the machine-cut. Generally speaking, the more modern the style, the more likely it is that the pendants have been machine-cut.

Metalwork also gives an indication of the workmanship of the chandelier. But it is hard to remember to look at that amidst the blaze and sparkle of the crystal.

In antiques the metalwork may be the key to the value of the entire piece. For instance, old Russian chandeliers are judged almost exclusively by the hand detailing, chasing, and applied decoration. The same criteria can be used to judge modern pieces, although the English-style frames are often made of glass instead of metal.

Lighting from a chandelier is usually not enough to do the entire illumination job. Or, if it is, there is the danger of a too-bright light in the center of the room and too sharp a contrast with shadows. The chandelier wasn't designed to do the entire lighting chore alone, so it's best not to demand that. Instead, you should add lights, such as candles on the table or sconces on the wall to eliminate glare and shadows. Small spotlights in the ceiling that illuminate the walls and even the chandelier itself can make a big difference between having a brilliant illumination and having a beautiful setting.

There's another item that has to be considered in the setting—color. But whether anything can be done about it is another matter. As of this moment, if appliance sales are an indication, 9 million American housewives are surveying their beige living rooms and yellow kitchens with great distaste and complaining: "This house is worn out. We've got to refurnish."

And 9 million husbands, preparing for defeat, are groaning: "Worn out? But we just got new upholstery and draperies a couple of years ago. And the kitchen is practically new."

Of all the factors that go into making a setting and keeping it, none is so powerful as the use of color. Psychology tells us that the eye sees what it is used to seeing. And when that changes—well, to quote a buyer for the B. Altman department stores, "When a room looks drab, dated, and in urgent need of redoing, it's usually because the color is out of style." If you're keeping score at home, beige upholstery and yellow appliances, which were in style six or seven years ago, are now out. In their place, as a look in the stores reveals, are avocado green and gold. "They may not be the colors people want," says a retail store home furnishings stylist who prefers to remain anonymous. "But when there's enough of a color around, people will buy the story. It's a sort of a brainwashing job."

This assault comes from every direction, according to the Color Association of the United States. A change in color comes as a barrage from everybody, from upholstery and clothing fabric makers to auto interior stylists, packagers, and supermarket suppliers. Moreover, you can hardly turn around these days without running into a bombardment of words as well—"decorator colors," "color coordination," "color styling," and a host of other reminders to get with the current hue. But what *is* current? If beige and yellow look drab and worn out now, refurnishing in up-to-date avocado and gold is hardly a reasonable exercise in foresight. A spot check reveals that big fabric houses are beginning to think about retooling for a change to muted colors—grays, taupes and tweeds—within the next three years or so. But there seems to be very little advantage to knowing that because, as a spokesman for Greef fabrics told me recently, "Turquoise is already on the horizon, although it may take a while to get here."

All of this rapid change in color setting is quite new. Until the early 1950s a color style could be expected to last nearly a decade. The 1920s, for example, lived very comfortably with royal blue and burgundy. The 1930s got along nicely on Williamsburg blue and dusty pink. The 1940s took up forest green and flame red along with khaki and blue serge . . .

And then came 1948, when a decorating magazine, assuming the position of spokesman-for-color for 96 participating manufacturers, published its first annual color report and forecast. This was—and is—an attempt by the magazine to establish a uniform list of the names and hues that home furnishings manufacturers will be using during the year, in an effort to save the consumer agony in matching colors. A particular shade of green, for example, and the name "Lettuce," will then be available in all sorts of furnishings, from refrigerators to drapery fabric. When the marketplace has been saturated with a color, the magazine usually gets its participating manufacturers to drop it and its name from production. Today, there are over 600 manufacturers who coordinate their color-and-name activities through this important magazine's annual color program.

"Plan for continuity and surprise with matching floors and walls," the magazine said in its first report in 1948, calling on behalf of its members-in-color for a choice from among serene green-blues, forest green, avocado, and a few accents of flame and pink. In all, about 20 colors were forecast. And whatever changes were introduced, they left the 1940 setting—and the eye that was used to it—undisturbed.

Two years later, however, the color report and forecast for the coming year indicated a few surprises. For 1951 it was going to be yellow with black and white, green with black and white, yellow and red. But within five years, red was out. In fact, in 1955, the heyday of psychological testing, startling colors and combinations were out. According to the forecast reported by participating manufacturers, it was going to be a world of pastels. If you like red you ought to have your head examined. But in 1960 the forecast was talking about brilliant and high-spirited colors for the coming year. And, as a further break with recent tradition, more than three colors per room were predicted. In addition, for the first time in several decades, prints appeared.

Another five years passed, and with it another recent tradition. In 1965 the color forecast was "away from brilliant color schemes, away from showcase rooms that dominate the people who live in them." In other words, back to the serenity of 1950. But it didn't work out that way. The color machine that had been building in textile design rooms and appliance factories was now in business for itself. And paying no attention to the driver who was trying to get back to serenity, color settings marched forward into the psychedelics. In 1970, with 600 participating manufacturers and a catalog of almost 40 colors to choose from, the magazine made no forecast.

The result of this rapid change and increasing bombardment of color has had a very powerful effect on both the home setting and the eye that looks at it. A look into this kaleidoscopic world of stylists, chemists, and marketers turns up some very disquieting information:

➔Color is the single most important selling item today. People are ready to sacrifice quality for color, "even in many things that must actually do work, such as pots, pans and other cookware," says an editor at this same magazine, whose job it is to cover the retailing scene.

➔In some fibers, especially synthetics, certain colors mean a weakened or less stable fabric. "This one," says a textile executive, holding up a hank of yarn, "now is available in brighter colors. But to do that, we've had to decrease its ability to withstand the effects of sunlight. This color won't last the way darker colors do."

➔In many items, the need to put out a full line of colors means additional cost of production—a cost that is naturally passed on to the consumer.

➔But just as important as these tangible, quantitative changes brought on by the whirling color machine is the havoc it has caused in the world of taste and beautiful things. "It used to be," said a home furnishings stylist at a New York department store, "that our customers could roam around and find a chair or a table they liked. Granted, it was a haphazard approach. But they weren't being influenced by a 'look' or a total arrangement.

"But in this world of every color available, we've had to arrange our displays, or else have our customers get dizzy with the wild look of a haphazard placement. And so now, with the 'total look' approach, we've been able to sell some really ugly things because they can't be seen as entities anymore. For example, who would want to own a dozen black wine goblets? But when you see a display table in the store set with a red cloth, green napkins, white plates, yellow candles and black goblets, the whole look is rather effective. We've sold a lot of black goblets that way. But it was the only way. When they were displayed alone, they were just a dozen black goblets, and naturally nobody wanted them."

So, the vast variety and annual change in color coordination has made for less flexibility rather than more in today's setting. From black wine goblets to white vinyl modern furniture, everything appears to depend on a very carefully constructed "total look." For all of its horsehair, hidebound rules, and regulations, the Victorian setting was no more rigid and demanding.

Whether there's a way out of this straitjacket is very hard to say. But investing in a total look does not seem to be the route for most people of average means. Consequently, there is only one thing to do—and that is to take it home, whatever it is, and see how it fits into the setting you have created. That's not as easy to do as it is to say, of course. Asking the eye to calm down is asking a lot. But there is no alternative except to buy the styles and colors you used to have, in the faith and hope that the pendulum of taste will swing back your way. That is, if the styles and colors you used to have are available. But don't bet on it.

XI

How Consumers Are
Manipulated in the
Marketplace

ATTIC Recent? Antique Modern? Buy a painter? Sooner or later anybody who invests in beautiful things will have to come to grips with the question of "Will they still be beautiful tomorrow, or the day after?"

It is this worry that accounts in large part for the thriving traffic in antiques, the theory being that if an object has survived half a century or two, then it has been endowed by time with an intrinsic value and is worth living with. But that does not answer the question of whether it is beautiful and whether it will stay that way. Many coveted antiques on the market today were either considered monstrosities by the taste leaders of their day, or else held in contempt for being below proper standards. An eighteenth-century pewter pitcher, for example, commands handsome prices today. But in its own time it would not have been seen on the table of any home concerned with beautiful things. In those days, pewter bespoke lower-middle-class ideals. It was considered the tableware of people who had graduated from using wooden utensils but who were not yet up to sterling silver or even rolled Sheffield plate.

On the other hand, just because an object is made in a new design, that does not insure its enduring beauty. Those very chic butterfly chairs of 15 or 20 years ago—a canvas or leather hammock slung low on a bent iron rod frame— they're not the things of beauty they used to be, and they may never become so again even in a century or two. So looked at that way, an investment in antiques is not necessarily an investment in beauty. And conversely, buying what is in and discarding what is out is a very extravagant way to invest and it really solves only the problem of day-to-day fashion. But whether it is beautiful today and will still be so tomorrow is another kind of question.

To answer it accurately, of course, would require the ability to see into the future, and that is a very rare talent. But inasmuch as the future is rooted in the past, a good part of the answer can be found by looking backward and re-phrasing the question, to ask, "Was it beautiful yesterday— and if it isn't still beautiful today, why not?" In other words, how have our ideals changed and what are the principles to be learned from that process of change?

It's not necessary to look all the way back to the temples of ancient Greece or the court of Louis xiv to document a real change in taste. All you have to do is look over your shoulder at the American Sunday dinner one short generation ago, and compare it with today's.

To begin with the place setting, a generation ago the average middle-class set of "company" silver was silver plate. Sterling was sold mostly to the carriage trade, according to the Sterling Silversmith's Guild of America. But today, that is no longer true. Sterling flatware is now middle-class "company" silver. In the past year sterling flatware sales rose 50 percent over the year before. On the other hand, sales of plated flatware are off, and dropping annually. The second or "everyday" flatware is usually stainless steel these days. And as for the kind of sterling bought today, one of the largest and oldest silver companies has had to discontinue its line of lightweight low-cost flatware because it hasn't been selling anywhere near as well as the more expensive, heavier, higher quality sterling.

Moreover, a generation ago there was a great flurry of excitement over the newly developed plastic dishes and plates, synthetic fabrics on floor and upholstered dining room chairs, and those "hard-wearing table tops that look just like polished wood," to quote an advertisement of that day. But that has changed, too. According to a survey of middle-class housewives conducted by a major consumer magazine, the American woman these days prefers china or pottery to plastic dishes; linen, silk, or wool, even if she can't yet afford them, to synthetic fabric upholstery; and wood furniture. Today, furniture companies using plastics to imitate wood are quite timid about announcing that matter to shoppers.

The decoration of the dining room has changed apace. A generation ago the middle-class family that could afford it had wall-to-wall carpeting on the floor—the same one-color carpeting that covered the other rooms and stairs. On the walls there was very likely to be a print of flowers in an oval frame, or a copy of the *Laughing Cavalier* or *The Calmady Children* or, in more adventurous homes, a print of a Van Gogh. Today that middle-class dining room has pulled up the wall-to-wall carpeting and has put down an Oriental or a Scandinavian rug, but in any case there is plenty of wood to be seen. On the wall it is entirely possible to find a reproduction of a Picasso, or a Chagall, Cézanne, etc., if not an original piece of art. It is also quite possible that those have been either painted by a member of the family or rented from a local museum. And on the sideboard—kept bare a generation ago or decorated with only a pair of candlesticks—there is apt to be a model reproduction of a piece of sculpture by Rodin or Michelangelo. Manufacturers of these reproductions, which are usually sold through museums and department stores, report sales up nearly 20 times over what they were two decades ago. And the Museum of Modern Art in New York says that it receives four or five requests daily from other museums across the country asking for information on setting up a painting-rental department.

A generation ago, of course, there was no silver coffee or tea service, or silver plate, either. And today's dining room probably doesn't have one—yet. But in a recent survey, middle-class women overwhelmingly said that they wanted that sugar-creamer-pot-and-tray because it would definitely "demonstrate beauty and elegance" in the home. That aspiration was not to be found in the dining room of a generation ago. Elegance was not a widely worked part of the vocabulary of that time. In its stead was "functional." The dining room was easily served, easily cleaned and, when possible, folded up and stored until the next company dinner. In those days not so long ago, to judge from the advertisements and picture stories of the time, middle-class homes and apartments were built with either a small dining room or, frequently, with only an alcove off the living room to serve the purpose. Today's generation does not accept that blueprint. According to statistics gathered from the building and furniture trades, today's householder wants a full-sized dining room because—to quote one survey—"it encourages conversation, enthusiasm, and a festive family feeling."

Last but far from least in the catalog of changed taste is the Sunday menu itself. A generation ago it was either dinner out in a restaurant or, if at home, then: roast stuffed chicken, mashed potatoes, and string beans or peas. If wine was served at all (it probably wasn't), it was a sauterne. Dessert, naturally, was a pie—apple, peach, or berry.

Well, the baby in the high chair at that dinner is a grown woman now, with small children of her own. Her company menu today will very likely include chicken, but it will be chicken cooked with wine or oranges or almonds. More likely, Sunday dinner will be beef bourguignon, sauteed mushrooms, and artichoke hearts. There will almost certainly be wine, perhaps Châteauneuf-du-Pape. And for dessert: chocolate mousse.

The evidence for this sort of change in taste abounds— not only in the sales statistics of pastry brushes, tart shells, souffle dishes, and other gourmet cooking utensils, but also in the import figures for French table wines (not including champagne), which are up 400 percent over 1960. Books about wines and their use are selling apace, with one encyclopedia on the subject priced at $15 and doing four times the business of its nearest competitor, priced at $5.95. But the most vivid evidence of a change in palate over the past generation can be found in the business of cookbooks today.

A generation ago there were three or four standard texts for the preparation of meals, such as *The Settlement House Cook Book* and *The Fanny Farmer Cook Book.* Today there are 1,536 different titles in print, covering the cuisine of almost every nation and area in the world, as well as the favorite recipes of statesmen, tycoons, celebrities—or the people who knew them personally. To a casual observer in this land of Julia Child, Craig Claiborne, James Beard, Michael Field, and Annemarie (a girl who once worked for Jacqueline Kennedy and has written a cookbook about her experiences), there appear to be only three approaches to cuisine not yet compiled: *The Lemon Cook Book* (a complete guide to dishes that are either lemon-flavored or yellow-colored);

The Stir Cook Book (1,000 favorite recipes by the inmates of Alcatraz); and *The Egg Cream Trauma* (what the most-prepared dishes in America *really* mean according to the nation's leading psychiatrists, with an introduction by Lucy Freeman).

Suffice it to say that ideals of beauty and the good life have changed visibly between the last generation and this. Which ideal is the more enduring is impossible to say without taking a look at one more change. But it is worth noting that the management of the best-known *haute cuisine* restaurants in New York admit that their dinner business is now in direct competition with meals made at home.

The Sunday dinner of a generation ago, of course, was a change from that of two generations before it. That older era was the tag-end of the Late Victorian period. Many middle-class homes had electric light, some had automobiles, a few had telephones.

In the dining room, however, there was general agreement about taste and beauty. The tablecloth was white satin damask. On the wall hung pastoral prints and an oil portrait or two of family members. The sideboard was dark and heavy, faced with intricate carving that needed constant dusting. On top was the coffee or tea service, perhaps a piece of cut crystal or glass and, if possible, an oriental-style vase or bowl. The carpet was almost certainly a Brussels with a flowered or figured pattern. In the window, colored glass, and the same for the shade over the table light.

But the keynote of the large, dark, crowded room was the flatware. Whether silver plate or sterling, there were at each place setting a profusion of forks, knives, spoons, spears, spreaders—at the very least six or seven, plus the utensils that came to the table with dessert. To a stranger from a later time, it appeared to be much more than a piece for each course—and it was. For that older generation, Sunday dinner (and, in fact, most weekday dinners) was a ritual carried on with the proper etiquette. There were rules, regulations, and niceties in the conduct of a meal, and they were observed to the letter of propriety.

For the generation that followed, a functional dining room—and household—seemed to be not only a daring break with the past but also an important step forward into progress and sanity. It was only natural to pull up the stylized Brussels and put down a businesslike Axminster. It was only reasonable to take off the velvet plush upholstery and cover the dining room chairs in washable plastic. It was more than logical—it was absolutely necessary to dispense with the dust-catching carved furniture and light-blocking colored glass and replace them with more practical materials. And as for the matter of etiquette, that book was removed from the kitchen shelf and replaced with several on the subject of good nutrition.

What happened to all those discards and rejects left over when the Late Victorian taste and ideal of beautiful things was supplanted? Well, after 60 years of storage in the attic of bad taste, most of them are back in favor again. That includes such items as stained glass windows, serpentine love seats, heavily inlaid woodwork, horsehair, velvet plush, and all the rest of what was considered only yesterday to be a dark, cumbersome, rigid style of living. And the proof of it is that the dusty old housewrecking and building demolition industry has become a thriving boutique in the home furnishings market.

Recently in one such boutique—a housewrecking company's warehouse in Stamford, Connecticut—behind a bulldozer and a concrete bear that once guarded a bank door and carries the number 1903, stood an intricately carved walnut fireplace mantel and a matching mirror frame of the sort that William Howard Taft might have looked into.

"How much do you want for that pair?" a customer inquired.

"Well," the salesman in overalls said hesitantly, "we're asking $200."

"Ridiculous," the customer snapped. "You can get at least $500, and maybe more."

That kind of scene is being played in similar boutiques across the United States. As the salesman later explained: "How am I supposed to know what this stuff is worth? My business is pulling old buildings down. When it comes to selling off the salvage, I've got to go by what the customers tell me. But they're very helpful. Did you know that you could get as much as 5 cents a square foot for old stamped tin ceilings . . . ?"

Just what this generation sees in that generation's ceilings is impossible for the in-between generation to understand. It will be equally hard for them to make sense out of the following spot-check of housewreckers:

In Chicago, weather-beaten concrete eagles weighing a ton or more are outselling concrete bears by three to one. That, it seems, is a reversal of last year's trend. When the Pittsburgh National Bank was demolished recently, whole families armed with hatchets came to take out the marble flooring, paying 50 cents a square foot for the privilege. One family also paid $8,000 to take away the entire board room. In New York, sinks from a 1905 jail went for $20 each, and marble stairs and bannisters from old movie houses—temples to the Late Victorian ideal—have gone for $1,000 at the very least. In New Jersey, cement gargoyles used as rainspouts on turn-of-the-century office buildings have brought as much as $250.

All of that, of course, is in addition to the thriving antique shop market in Victorian art, decoration, and furnishings. "Until a year or two ago we didn't bother with Victoriana," an executive of a large auction house said. "It just wasn't worth the time. We simply shipped it down South where they loved it because they live in the past. But now we put it on the block in every large city with very, very gratifying results." Dealers in Late Victorian silver plate—electroplated, not old Sheffield—have also seen prices skyrocket. The boom in Tiffany glass, as well as modern copies of it, bears additional witness to this renaissance of an era that was until very recently scorned. But the real seal of approval from the good taste establishment was placed on the ideals of two generations ago when the Museum of Modern Art mounted a show of art nouveau, that frilly, festooned, and filigreed style of the turn of the century. At the same time, the Metropolitan Museum of Art ran an acres-long exhibition called "19th Century America" signifying in no uncertain terms that it was all right to have regard for Victoriana—Early, Mid, and Late. As a spokesman for the Metropolitan Museum told me, "The nineteenth century has been very much misunderstood and should be reappraised."

Now, this is not to say that the revival in the taste of that time reflects everybody's taste today, or is even one of the four walls of this generation's temple of beauty. Far from it. That fact was easily established by anybody who cared to eavesdrop on conversations in the Metropolitan's Nineteenth-Century exhibition. Said one woman in her seventies to a companion of about the same age: "How can they charge admission to a show like this? It's dreadful stuff, and I knew it when I was growing up in it." Said a man of 50 or so to his teen-aged son: "Now that room setting over there—that's exactly how my grandmother's dining room looked. She was your great-grandmother. I always felt that the portieres were

going to reach out and suffocate me." The only real enthusiasm seemed to come from people in their 20's and early
30's. One young woman said to a man who might have been
her husband, "Why, that stained glass window is just like the
one we got for the dining room window . . ."

It is not only a matter of age that separates those who
approve of this kind of taste from those who don't. People
whose careers are built on the taste business also disagree
about the Late Victorian ideal of beauty. Many not only sell
these relics and their copies, but also welcome the revival of
what one dealer called "a more understandable time if not a
happier one." But on the other hand, one of the biggest
wholesalers in antiques in the United States said irritably
that he "hated Victorian stuff, always had, always would. It's
unpleasant to look at it. And it's simply not good taste. It
can't be." A manufacturer of high-priced, high quality furniture said: "If it's a trend, then this firm will not be a part of
it. We will continue to carry reproductions of eighteenth-
century pieces. If we handle any nineteenth century, it will
be only their reproductions of the eighteenth." And, added a
decorator whose work frequently illustrates the house-and-
home magazines: "Victoriana may be interesting historically.
But really, I can't have my name and reputation associated
with interiors that are filled with that kind of nonsense."

Under the circumstances, it is very hard to say for certain whether those things of two generations ago are beautiful today. But it is equally hard to say just how beautiful
they were in their own time. True enough, they sold well—
especially the plated silver, because the discovery of new, vast
lodes put the metal, or at least a coating of it, within the
reach of the middle class. But Charles Eastlake, the most
widely read critic of home furnishings taste of the time, explained to his avid audience:

"A large proportion of modern silver is stamped in patterns which have no more artistic quality than the ornaments of a wedding cake. Take, for instance, the ordinary 'fiddle pattern' fork. Can anything be more senseless than the way in which modifications of that form are decorated—now with a raised molding at its edge, now with an outline of beads, now with what is called a 'shell,' now with a rococo scroll or representation of natural flowers . . .

"People buy them because there is nothing else of the kind to be had. But there is no more art in their design than there is in that of a modern bedpost."

It is worth noting that Late Victorian bedpost beds are selling very nicely on the antique market these days. It is also worth noting that next to the cookbook, the most wide-selling book on household management today is the encyclopedia of etiquette. It's not the same volume that was consulted two generations ago, of course. But it is the same sort of guide for the perplexed, and marks another visible change from the taste and ideals of a generation ago when it was usually a book on money management or on vitamin requirements that stood on the shelf.

All of these changes noted, it remains only to examine the process of that change in hopes of answering the question: "If it's beautiful today, will it still be beautiful tomorrow and the day after?"

Generally speaking, a generation usually takes its name from the activity or person bespeaking the taste and ideals of its time. There is, for example, the cool and reasonably proportioned Federal period. There is the spacious and manicured Antebellum era. There is the prim and proper Late Victorian age. But those labels are only an approximation, a sort of shorthand to note some aspects of the way life was

organized at the time. During the cool and reasonably proportioned Federal period, for example, some of the country's
most unwieldy and labyrinthine city plans were devised. In
the spacious and manicured Antebellum era, small, dark,
airless town houses and office buildings were erected. And as
for the prim and proper Late Victorian day, that was the
younger generation responsible for what is now known by
the catch phrase "modern art."

Each of these neatly labeled generations also had their
antique collectors, avant-garde taste rebels, and wistful and
sharp-tongued critics yearning for a return to older, better
times and ideals. Looked at more closely, each "generation"
has been a medley of tastes if not an outright discordant
chorus of differences, ideals, and endeavors. At the very height
of Late Victorian academic painting and mass-produced furniture and decoration, the Impressionists were very much
alive and kicking, and all kinds of experiments in handcrafts
were underway.

The same is true of the present generation, regardless of
what name posterity gives it. The fabric of our taste is woven
of many kinds of yarn, some old, some synthetic, some simply
hasty patches. We appear to be affluent and seem to have two
of everything—two phones, two cars, two homes, and frequently two marriages. And it does not surprise us in the
least that one phone is as modern in design as a spaceship
while the other, also considered a work of art, is a French
model, circa 1928. Nor is it surprising to see a family buy a
Tudor style house in the suburbs and a Cape Cod cottage or
an aluminum-welded mobile home in the country. Without
violating any of his principles regarding taste and beauty,
a man today will commit $5,000 or more to own both a sleek,
pointed sedan and a boxy, snub-nosed second car.

Over the dining room table today may hang a colored
glass lamp shade whose ancestry can be traced to the turn of

the century, or a crystal chandelier whose prototype was built when the Bastille was fully occupied. But over the piano, deep set into the ceiling, may be a pair of spotlights invented not so long ago for office building lobbies. Behind the living room easy chair may stand a tree of lamps whose prototype was used in department store windows. And as for the chair itself, if it's one of those immense leather jobs on a stainless steel base, then it is the direct descendant of the chair designed and reserved for corporation officers.

Like every period before it, this one is in transition. A look at the booming business in etiquette books tells that story quite plainly. "When Emily Post wrote her book," said Elizabeth Post, who has revised and modernized the original, "she was talking to society people. I am talking to the middle class. The new edition talks about driving etiquette, applying for jobs, dealing with the handicapped, and so on. I left the chapter on 'Household Help' in the new edition as a museum piece." In Amy Vanderbilt's revised edition, she deals with "problems thought unprintable when the first edition came out in 1952." These include such matters as how to extend a proper invitation to a homosexual couple, socializing between the black and white races, and the amount of freedom a college girl should have under her parents' roof compared with the kind of morality acceptable on the campus. A third etiquette book, aimed specifically at teenagers, takes up the properties of seating arrangements for divorced parents and their separate families. A fourth book deals with the proper way to word the wedding announcement when the bride holds a doctor's degree and the groom does not.

So, that's the first and most important principle regarding taste—namely that it changes from generation to generation.

The second principle is that nobody belongs to a "generation." That is a term best left to genetics, history, and sociology. Properly speaking, people live lifetimes. And whether an object that is beautiful in this one will still be beautiful in the next lifetime is a question not worth a moment's consideration.

That leads directly to the third principle. If it's beautiful, it will usually last a lifetime. Selecting beautiful things is a creative endeavor, and creativity is enduring. Selecting beautiful things is also self-expression—or it should be—and that is enduring as well. If you delegate the exercise of taste to experts or survey statistics, however, you run a terrible risk. Experts and averages seldom last a lifetime.

The fourth and last principle of beauty and its durability should go without saying, but perhaps it cannot in this age of marketing and taste-making. And that is, there is not just one beautiful thing. There are many—antique, second-hand, spanking new. But just because it's new or very old, that doesn't necessarily make it beautiful. To quote Charles Eastlake again, writing a century ago about many new objects of his time that have become antiques in ours:

"When did people first adopt the monstrous notion that the last pattern out must be the best? Is good taste so rapidly progressive that every mug which leaves the potter's hands surpasses in shape the last which he molded?

"This absurd love of change—simply for the sake of change—is even now carried to such an extent that if one desires to replace a jug or a table cloth with another of the same pattern, even a few months after the first has been bought, it is extremely difficult, sometimes impossible to do so. The answer is always the same: 'Last year's goods, sir. We couldn't match them now.' "

XII

How the Consumer Can Protect Herself

THE organ peals. The church bells, too. And amid the rice and good wishes another bride and groom begin the endlessly creative adventure of furnishing their lives with beautiful things.

At least that's one way of looking at it. Another view, more popular in certain quarters, goes this way:

The cash register rings. The checkbook snaps. And amid the receipts and down payments, another couple of big spenders joins the economy.

According to banking and merchandising statistics today's bride and groom spend an average of $3,000 on setting up housekeeping in the three months before and the three months after the wedding ceremony. At an average age of 23.3, they account for $5 billion in annual sales of furniture, china, flatware, rugs, and the like. Never again, the statistics show, will today's newlyweds be able to invest in so many beautiful things so fast. But, being so young, their taste in most of their investment will change by the time they approach the age of 30—requiring a long and steady outlay of money to replace their original purchases.

This young couple is a different species from their parents and grandparents, who invested in beautiful things piece by piece over many years. But this new species is no accident of nature. This new approach to investing in beautiful things didn't just happen. On the contrary, the change in attitude has been brought about by a number of observable forces and currents.

This new attitude goes by the name of consumerism, and it can be seen at work as early as the elementary and junior high school levels. It is best summed up by the head of the home economics department of a large Pennsylvania city school system, who explained: "Our students are much more concerned with 'how to buy' these days than with 'how to make,' as their parents were." The extent of this change in teaching youngsters the ways of the world can be readily documented in the consumer education departments of many large manufacturing companies and trade associations in the United States today.

A cursory glance into the home economics office of a suburban junior high school, for example, shows shelves piled high with teaching materials supplied by Household Finance Corp., Oneida silver, General Electric, Kroehler furniture, Campbell soups, Sachs stores, and so on. The Monsanto chemical people report that their quarterly newsletter, covering their own products as well as general information about the marketplace, goes to more than 10,000 home economists and teachers across the nation. Burlington Industries has recently set up a department of consumer affairs headed by Letitia Baldridge, former social secretary to Jacqueline Kennedy Onassis. As a first step, Burlington's new consumer education department has queried thousands of home economists, asking them what kinds of teaching aids, materials, and information would benefit them. In reply, they have received about 500 letters per month.

Taken all together, "how to buy" education has vastly outweighed the old-fashioned "how to make" teaching that once shaped schoolchildren's standards of taste and quality. That is not to say the "how to buy" approach is wrong—most especially in this era of plastics, synthetics, and super mass production that can make things much less expensively and sometimes much better than the old handmade variety. But just what kinds of lessons are taught in consumerism is another matter. In school films supplied by manufacturing firms, associations, and trade groups, the range of titles is certainly broad enough—from "How to Select Furniture" produced by Sears Roebuck to "The Romance of Gloves" from the National Association of Leather Glove Manufacturers. But a viewing of the film does not always provide a hearty and nutritious table of contents.

One film, for example, made for schoolroom use by a large fiber-producing company, seemed at first very complete, showing the whole range of synthetics now being used in carpeting. You certainly came away feeling that you had learned a lot. But could you remember the information? Or, as it seemed later, did you find yourself bathed in the after-image of rugs that were chic, glamorous, and possibly just the thing to have on your kitchen floor? "Possibly that is the after-image," said an executive in the company that produced the film. "But it's a small price to pay for a free film that helps a home economics teacher explain the complexities of today's living to the youngsters."

Whether it has to be that complex depends a great deal on whether you are a consumer or a supplier. There is, it appears, considerable profit to be made in confusion—as anyone can find out by following up a few of those educational films about the world of plastics and synthetics in order to find out how to buy fabric and furniture—the disadvantages as well as the advantages. That is not an idle inquiry in today's consumer market, where more than half of the nation's 6,000 furniture manufacturers are using at least some plastic in their products, and the sale of synthetic fibers climbed by 1.4 billion pounds last year over the year before, while the sale of wool remained about the same.

For the consumer, conditioned to seeing the market as terribly complex and looking at his buying as a purchase rather than an investment, there are three courses open in his quest for information.

One course is to abandon it completely and stick to buying only natural fibers and materials. But more and more, each day wood becomes either a luxury item or the low end of the furniture line. And at the same time, it gets harder and harder to find linen, cotton, or wool used alone rather than in combination with man-made fibers.

The second route through the complexity is to read the labels carefully and go by what they say. But what do they say? In furniture made totally or partially of plastic, the label often says simply, "pecan finish" or "walnut finish." And even if the label were to say "High Impact Draculite," what would that mean? In fabric, and most especially in clothing, the label must tell you the precise content of the fibers. But what about the properties of the combination—how do they wear, how do they clean, how do they compare with others?

The third course for a consumer in the plastics and synthetics marketplace is to take his inquiry to the manufacturer, the weaver, the producer of the basic chemicals. That, as it turns out, is where the "complexities of today's life" originate largely. And quite often profitably.

<hr />

"The poor consumer. He has a tough job. He can't tell a thing just by looking."

Those are the words of Charles Redfern of the Plastics Industries, Inc., of Tennessee. And they are an understatement for anybody looking either at the plastic and synthetic wares in the marketplace, or to their makers and producers for information. In plastic furniture, it turns out that industry associations and manufacturers' groups have very little information about care, buying, or differences in the various types of materials being used today. In the area of synthetic fibers, the producers aren't terribly interested in talking to the consumer at all. "And why should they?" asked a spokesman for a large textile company. "Why should they want to talk to the consumer? Fiber producers don't have anything to sell to the consumer. They sell to textile people."

Makers of the basic plastic chemicals used in furniture production aren't much interested in talking to consumers, either. "What good does information do a person shopping for furniture?" asked a representative of a titanic plastics producing corporation. "Let's say that a customer is looking for a Spanish style table. What's the point in his knowing that the legs are polystyrene, the geegaws are polyurethane, and the top is a laminate? Even if he knows that, how does he know something hasn't gone wrong in the manufacturing of the piece? Maybe the legs will split and the top will crack. And the materials might not be to blame at all."

Well, if knowing about the product and how it is made isn't the answer, what is? "Trust the manufacturer to make a good product," said an executive with another plastics corporation. "And trust the store to stand behind the product, too. The salesman can tell the consumer everything he has to know."

The reply to that formula can be made by citing three items from the synthetic fabric market. To wit:

ITEM. A woman in New Orleans bought a $675 acetate velvet evening coat last year. She wore it once—on a rainy night—and discovered later that the spots left by rain would not come out. The cleaner said he didn't know why. The store said it wasn't the fault of the merchandise, and would not credit her account until she threatened to sue.

ITEM. A suburban Pennsylvania woman bought a $200 spring coat made by a bonding process that laminates the front to the backing by heat. After one trip to the dry cleaner's the coat developed air bubbles between the bonded layers making it unwearable. This woman is now suing both the store and the dry cleaner.

ITEM. A $400 crepe wool dress came back from the cleaner's with its buttons melted and the drippings sealed for eternity into the fabric. The cleaner told the irate customer that he had no idea the plastic buttons would act that way, and he offered to replace them. A spokesman for the store where she bought the dress told her: "Everybody knows you have to remove the buttons before you have this sort of dress cleaned. It's your maid's responsibility to do that." And the more-than-irate husband, whose income doesn't provide for a maid, said, "What the hell are plastic buttons doing on a $400 dress!" It was a rhetorical question. The real question is pending in the courts.

In these three cases, there was nothing wrong with the product—except a lack of information regarding care and cleaning. And there are thousands of cases like these regarding dozens of different items. Just how far the store will stand behind its merchandise, of course, depends on the particular store, the particular object, and the way the customer asks for reimbursement. But when it comes to asking sales people for the information you need to know—well, there were three frequent replies given: (1) "We've sold a lot of them this week, so they must be all right"; (2) "Bonding is wonderful. Look at how lightweight this coat is"; and (3)

"Look at the label. See who made the fiber? I'm sure there's no need to worry."

In the world of synthetic fibers and fabrics, there are all sorts of valid reasons for not putting permanent information into sewn-in labels. According to a fiber manufacturer's representative: "The fiber producer doesn't always know how his yarns will be used, or with what other fibers it may be combined." According to a spokesman for a textile mill that combines the fibers with others to make fabric, "If our yardage is to be used in clothing, we don't know what kinds of buttons, thread, stiffening, or zipper will be used in the final manufacture." According to one good-sized garment manufacturing firm: "The fabric houses will promise you anything until you've signed the contract to buy their goods. Then they tell you to read the small print in the contract. That's where you find out that they aren't responsible for anything."

Last but not least in this obstacle course in the way of information regarding care and cleaning of fabrics is the law which makes no specific requirements about the matter. "And how could it?" asked a fiber chemist. "If our labels were to say 'Wash in lukewarm water,' what does that mean? Lukewarm isn't specific. And how do you know what solvent each dry cleaning establishment is going to use? And if we specified the cleaning agent to be used, we'd be in restraint of trade. On the other hand, of course, if the Federal Trade Commission demands that we put in permanent and specific labels, we are ready to comply."

So, that leaves it up to the consumer to find out the facts for himself. And that can mean a pretty heavy toll in long distance calls, as a recent three-week inquiry into this matter proved. After being shunted from office to office on one try, the phone call to a fabric house was finally taken by a woman who said briskly: "What's the best synthetic fiber? Oh, they're all the same. You should make your selection on the basis of style." A query about polyester used in furniture began in New York, was shifted to Chicago, then back to New York, and finally to Chicago, where a voice replied: "I really don't know much about it. Have you tried our New York office?"

One fiber producer, it turned out, employed an expert to answer questions like these. "Well," the expert said, "rayon, nylon, and acetate are really of equal quality." But a salesman in an office furniture showroom disagreed. "If you used a rayon-cotton combination in upholstery, you'd find the cotton worn out in a year or so, and the rayon still intact." But an upholsterer disagreed. "The rayon will go first," he said, "and the cotton will be left."

Sooner or later the consumer will have to be told— whether it will take heat, cleaning fluid, furniture polish; what to do if it cracks, chips, breaks; whether the one priced at $600 is a better buy than the one priced at $750. Sooner or later that kind of information will have to be readily available, just as it is regarding oak, walnut, linen, and wool.

"Oh, it will be available eventually," one textile man said. "But not until two things happen. First, the government will have to set the specifications for manufacturers to follow. And second, the manufacturers will have to get their trade names known by everybody in the country. After all, why should you tell a customer how to buy and look after a product unless you're sure he's going to buy yours."

There is one further obstacle in the way of getting information to the consumer. In this age of buying rather than investing, it appears that the consumer may not want to be informed.

"A lot of people want us to run color pictures of the products we test," said a spokesman for the Consumer's Union, which reports on the entire retail market's wares. "They say that they don't want all the information we give about various products and degrees of acceptability. Motorcycle groups, for example, aren't interested in consumer education about the use of helmets for safety. They want to feel the wind rushing through their hair." The National Better Business Bureaus confirm that diagnosis. "When a customer calls up for our suggestion about a product or a service," a BBB official said, "he or she usually has made a decision first. All we're supposed to do is corroborate that decision. And if we don't, then the caller just stops listening."

In the buying of beautiful things there is ample evidence that information about quality also falls on deaf ears. In fact the whole topic of value and worth has been bypassed in a number of items:

ITEM. Ten years ago Ed Spires was a window designer—a member of the decorating specialty that puts the feeling of opulence into department store window displays. "And then one day," he recalled, "it occurred to me that there might be a bigger market for this type of opulence." Today Spires is doing a thriving business in ancient tapestries, antique statues, and old paintings—which he makes in a small factory one flight up from his store.

ITEM. Ten years ago Ken Lane was a shoe designer working on a newly decorated model when, as he put it, "I saw what could be done with gems in new settings." Today the name of Kenneth J. Lane is celebrated from coast to coast and in London, Paris, and Rome for his mastery of counterfeit jewels—costing from $10 to $100.

ITEM. Ten years ago fake fur was either "fun" or "poor taste," depending on your brand of snobbery. Today several of the largest department stores have watched sales rise to compete vigorously with those of cloth coats.

ITEM. The synthetic fiber industry, surveying its sales figures, can report that the East Coast and West Coast will sacrifice durability for style. The Middle West, still clinging to what one fabric salesman calls "old fashioned ideas," is known in the trade as "nylon country."

ITEM. Not so long ago, no proper middle-class family would be caught with fake flowers on the table. It was either the real thing fresh from the garden or florist—or nothing. Today silk, paper, and plastic flowers are seen everywhere, including the White House. And wholesaler Vincent-Lippe is doing especially well in Florida where, a dealer explained, "It's so much less bother than having to go outside every day and cut fresh ones."

What accounts for this new breed, consumerism, that is no longer concerned with the hard facts of quality and real worth? In part, of course, it can be traced back to the taste leadership of stylists, decorators, and designers with their overwhelming accent on form. But there are other reasons as well.

According to Ed Spires, who had just finished making and selling a genuine fake thirteenth-century French chandelier for $32: "The people who buy these things are young, educated, well-read, well-traveled. But they don't have the money to buy originals, nor the desire to own copies and reproductions. They don't care if it's a fake. What they care about is the feel of the whole thing."

And, added fake gem designer Kenneth Lane, "Fake is now. People are free enough not to have to revere something just because it's real. Pearls aren't fun just because they're real. But just think about what you can do with a fake 30-carat emerald. Why, even the rich love to buy this stuff."

The rich seem to agree, to judge from Lane's clientele.

How to Invest in Beautiful Things

"It's wonderful." said Mrs. Nicholas Goulandris, wife of a Greek ship owner, who was looking over the latest fakes. "It's big, and it's flashy. There are no headaches with the insurance. And besides, you don't have to wear it next year if you don't want to."

That point of view is widespread enough to have consequences in the purchase and use of everything from motorcycle helmets and auto seat belts to tufted area rugs and black wine goblets. But regardless of how the fault is shared among maker, buyer, and merchandiser, the fact remains that the consumer is not armed and protected with information. So that leaves the job to professional watchdogs—private, governmental, and nonprofit.

At first look, it appears that no consumer in the history of buying and selling has ever had so many protectors working for him. The Federal government and several cities and states have bureaus of consumer affairs. Individual manufacturing firms, following the practice of retail stores, are setting up consumer complaint departments. The Better Business Bureaus and Consumer's Union are better subscribed to than ever. And some of Ralph Nader's associates have left Washington to start their own watchdog organizations in other parts of the country.

But the question remains: does all of this interest and activity mean better protection for the consumer? A spot check does not turn up a wonderfully satisfactory answer.

One nationally known department store with several suburban branches admits that its complaint department has a backlog of 4,000 unanswered letters from angry customers. A spokesman for a large association of retail stores hints darkly that many consumer watchdog organizations are out only to make trouble. "They're saboteurs," he said, "subversives—and worse." An enormous textile corporation, having announced proudly that it has now established a consumer affairs division, is asked to answer the charge that one of its fabrics is highly flammable. "That's not the concern of this office," a complaint division executive replied. And at the same time, a spokesman for the BBB—an efficient and effective mediator between buyer and seller—was saying, "The problem frequently is that the consumer doesn't know whom to complain to in the corporate hierarchy . . ." But if it's not the consumer affairs division and complaint officer, then who is it?

A look at the governmental machinery for protecting the customer isn't much more reassuring. In New York's much-publicized City Bureau of Consumer Affairs headed by former Miss America and TV personality Bess Myerson the problems appear to be summed up by Commissioner Myerson, who told me, "We could do so much better with a bigger budget. We could have more inspectors . . ." But a closer look reveals that some of the big obstacles can't be solved with money.

For one thing, there is the morass of an entrenched civil service that frequently does not take kindly to taking orders from bright young law school graduates and researchers who have been brought in to get the show on the road. There is, in addition, the very hard problem of legislation that confronts the Bureau. With great enthusiasm and hope recently the office called for unit pricing—telling stores to list the price-per-ounce, for example, instead of the price-per-box or price-per-bottle. As a way out of the maze of various-sized packages, it seemed a reasonable protection for the consumer. But it turned out that the law did not give the Bureau the authority for that order. And a suit by a group of store owners halted the practice. "We should have known better," said a young researcher.

In addition, there is the standard operating ailment common to most reform watchdog organizations, namely the tendency to draw too sharp a line between the good guys and the bad, between the weak and the strong. In one recent case the Bureau was implored by pushcart peddlers to extend their allowed territory of sales. But that, it turned out, would have been unfair competition for stores who, their owners explained, had rent, wages, and other fixed overhead costs.

There are also problems that arise in enforcing existing legislation. In one instance, the Bureau promised to clean up the used car business, beginning with an enforced 30-day guarantee on every auto sold. But that turned out to be too much protection for many consumers who wanted to buy a heap of junk and leisurely rebuild it in the back yard. A guaranteed car was more than they wanted or could afford.

Even in initiating consumer protection legislation there are built-in hazards. The New York City Bureau of Consumer Affairs recently got enacted what one staff lawyer called "a little Federal Trade Commission Act that will add immeasurably to our powers." But another lawyer on the city's payroll wondered what would happen when it came to enforcing the new law. "For example," he said, "what do the words in the new law 'unconscionable and deceptive' behavior actually mean?" He could see going to court if a consumer who speaks no English had signed a contract written in English and presented under false pretenses. But what about a case involving an antiques dealer who bought a warehouse full of secondhand silver in the United States, shipped the silver by plane to England, and sold it there to American tourists to take back home to the United States? Is that unconscionable and deceptive? Or is it only the rules of the game of buying and selling?

In the end, the real force of this particular watchdog government office lies in what Commissioner Bess Myerson calls "just being in existence." That not only keeps many makers and merchants in line, but it also educates consumers to the fact that they have rights, or should have. The clamor raised by the Bureau, for example, about unit pricing has resulted in the city finally making it a law.

Now, this is not to say that the buying public is unprotected, uninformed, unaware and—by tacit conspiracy—little more than a point-of-sale device. Far from it. True enough, there is no one voice to speak for the consumer, although there are choirs to sing of new designs, new products, new ideas, new packaging, and, of course, new credit cards. But that does not mean the consumer is mute. Not only does she write letters to reporters who cover the marketplace, but at lectures and group discussions she is very quick to speak her mind.

What she has to say could fill a book. And, in fact, this book is largely an answer to the more frequently asked questions. Her grievances, however, cannot be redressed in the same way. But it may be of more than passing interest to taste leaders and producers and merchandising specialists to know that she is angry.

Angry about what? A recent group discussion about the marketplace in a middle-sized city one hour by plane from New York and Chicago turned up comments like the following:

About decorating magazines: "I don't get anything out of them," said a woman married ten years. "The rooms always look beautiful. But they can't be translated into my needs."

Added another, "It seems to me that those magazines were a lot more helpful when they didn't use up so much of their space with advertising."

And said a woman in her early 40's: "My generation

read a magazine called 'Living for Young Homemakers.' We thought they were telling us how to furnish in style and quality. What a rude awakening to find out the truth. I no longer trust the magazines to tell me about buying things for my home."

About product quality: "I was assured by the store that the cotton-and-linen fabric for my couch was very hard-wearing. Well, in one year of use it is in need of reupholstering again," said one woman. "My family doesn't shop in that store anymore. And I've told all of my friends about this."

The woman sitting next to her added: "My family doesn't buy there anymore, either. My wall-to-wall carpeting is only three years old, and the steps are worn out. When I complained to the store, they turned me off with, 'what do you expect, with four people in your household.' "

About styling and design: "Manufacturers are so silly," said the wife of a hardware store owner. "They're afraid to let you know what drawbacks their products might have, and push the styling instead. When you find out the disadvantages for yourself, you stay away from their brand forever. Being conscious of trademarks is a double-edged sword."

Many of the women in the group expressed bitter complaints about what used to be open china and crystal patterns. "My pattern," said one, "had been standard since the turn of the century. But it's not available now. And when I wrote to the company about it, their attitude was, 'we're terribly sorry, but that's how the cookie crumbles.' "

Lamp and light fixture manufacturers came in for a great deal of criticism. "I can't believe," said one woman, "that only ugly lamps are being made. But those are the only ones I can find in the stores." And added another, "Why do lamp manufacturers make lamps that light only the lamp base instead of the room?"

About merchandising: "I've lived in a number of

cities," said the wife of a professor. "But unless you live in the very largest, you can't find out the extent of what is available. There's no place to see it except in catalogs. And I won't buy that way."

Another woman added, "Storekeepers don't want to take a chance on anything they haven't stocked before, even though they have a ready market for those things."

And, said a woman in her early 80's: "Now that the supermarkets and big shopping center palaces have driven out the small shopkeepers they can do as they please. That seems to mean medium to poor quality fruit and vegetables, mediocre meats, cheese that must be made out of plastic, and a general shoddy quality in the rest of the merchandise. So if you really care about how your home looks and what goes on your table, you have to spend your time combing the countryside for quality. I don't think we've really come very far in making and selling things since I was a bride."

Well, there is no need to go on with further evidence. Suffice it to say that the consumer is hardly unaware. And as the declining subscriptions to major magazines by the better potential consumers show, she is also unimpressed with the modern methods of merchandising. As for not wanting or not caring about information regarding products, one woman after another in discussion groups has told me in more or less the same words: "Of course I want the information. But I don't know where to get it." Quite a few have recounted long, discouraging tales of trying to make a complaint to the proper division of the manufacturer's executive office, and failing that, trying to find out a few facts about the product. In the end, they are all left with the old stand-by remedy that sometimes works and sometimes doesn't— namely, finding out the name of the president of the company and writing him directly to inquire or to complain. And, once the firm or store agrees to an adjustment or exchange or refund, they are then faced with having to begin the protest all over again in order not to have to pay credit charges.

But writing to the president of the company, and protesting credit charges, still leave the consumer fighting a hand-to-hand battle. And while she is becoming skilled at that sort of encounter, it still is not a fair fight, since a company or store can hold out a lot longer than she can. What the consumer lacks to even up the battle is organization. But that day is not far off when organized consumers can face organized business and industry.

In Philadelphia, for example, there is a five-year-old organization called the Consumer's Education and Protection Association. CEPA, as it is familiarly known, is a nonprofit, nongovernmental agency that believes no middleman can deal with the marketplace as effectively as the consumer himself when organized. Or, in the words of CEPA founder and director Max Weiner: "We believe in consumer power and the power of negative advertising. If the consumer can't get satisfaction out of court, then he has to do other things. Such as picket."

In its first five years of life, CEPA has helped about 4,000 individual consumers do these other things, and has been unsuccessful in only 5 percent of its attempts to help.

No manufacturer, retailer, or service organization is too big to tackle on behalf of an unhappy purchaser. CEPA has gone into battle against nationally known soup makers, mail order houses, and insurance companies, as well as local auto distributors, banks, credit firms, and public utilities. "We're not in business to picket," Weiner said. "But we are most effective that way. After all, to go to court over a $100 purchase can cost you as much as $1,000 in lawyers' fees—to say nothing of the months of waiting for the case to come up."

CEPA is a much less expensive way to have a complaint adjusted. The cost to the consumer is $2.

A number of business concerns have applied for membership in the organization. But naturally they have been turned down. As its name explains, CEPA is for the consumer. But no matter how big the case, or how sizable the victory, CEPA earns only $2 from each. And as Weiner pointed out, you can't really be at your best on a budget of $15,000. "What would work, however, would be a lot of local CEPA's all over the country. Not only would it help the consumer protection to have a national organization, but it would mean faster results. You could apply consumer pressure on both the local office and the home office, wherever it happened to be, at the same time."

One of the biggest $2 successes for CEPA since its founding was a recent campaign against a giant soup company that has been putting out a packaged breakfast. According to a test of the product made by Consumer's Union, the spices in the sausage were found to be infested with traces of vermin. While the U.S. government had found the level of contamination "acceptable," CEPA did not. And they picketed supermarkets in the Philadelphia area until the manufacturer replaced the spices in the packaged breakfast with spice oils.

Commenting on this campaign by CEPA and its outcome, a spokesman for the soup company told me: "We didn't have to take the product off the market. After all, the U.S. government had approved it. But we didn't want people to worry. There are more important things for people to worry about."

What they were he did not say.

Index

---‹¶{ *Index* }¶›---